READ TO SUCCEED

The Power of Books to Transform Your Life
& to Put You on the Path to Success

Stan Skrabut

REDSCORPION
PRESS

Read to Succeed:

The Power of Books to Transform Your Life and to Put You on the Path to Success

Copyright © 2018 by Stan Skrabut

All rights reserved.

Published by Red Scorpion Press

www.redscorpionpress.com

P.O. Box 289

Bemus Point, New York 14712

Contents

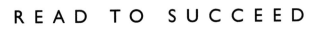

READ TO SUCCEED

Acknowledgments

Writing a book may seem like a solo project; however, a good book requires a committed team. This book would not have been possible without the following people.

I would first like to thank my wife, Bernadette van der Vliet. She has been a great support ever since I began talking about the idea. She read early drafts of the book and helped make each version better. She also shared her skills as a graphic designer to create a wonderful cover. Additionally, she created many graphics to support marketing the book. She has made me look better for over twenty-five years. I can't thank her enough.

Steve Miller is not only a great guy but a great editor. I gave him first crack at the book. Like previous projects I put in his hands, I got back a manuscript that was significantly better than when he received it.

The Red Scorpion Press team has been fantastic to work with. I want to single out Loren Mayshark, who believed in the project and took it on. His sound advice during all stages of the publishing process have helped make this book better. Many thanks to Vivian Lipari, who has spent many hours proofing various versions of the book. Each pass has helped produce a better product. I can't thank my launch team enough. This enthusiastic group of people has helped to spread the word about the project. They took a lot of weight off my shoulders as we got ready to launch. The success of this book launch is in a large part due to them. Thank you: Gary Chizever, Joe King, Joan Maddux, and Victor Villegas.

Introduction

Over and over, people have asked me why I wrote *Read to Succeed*. Frankly, I saw a disconnect between people who *wanted to be* successful and those who *were* successful. And I realized that those who were successful were reading books at a significantly higher rate than those who were struggling. As I explored this idea further, I discovered that some of the most successful people in history had developed a prominent reading habit.

I believe that people can increase their "luck" by developing a reading habit. Through a regular and sustained practice of reading books, you can become an expert on a topic by taking advantage of the coaching shared through books. Some of the most successful business leaders, including Bill Gates, Warren Buffett, Mark Cuban, and Elon Musk, set aside time to read as a way to generate new ideas. These ideas have contributed significantly to their success.

I want to help you develop a reading habit that will improve your chances for success. Many say they do not have time to read. However, President Theodore Roosevelt would read a book a day on a busy day and two to three books when he wasn't busy. He made it a priority and scheduled reading into his day.

Some say they get what they need from magazines or television. What a book provides over these other methods is a deep dive into a topic. You get expert knowledge presented in a neatly packaged resource. Mark Cuban says the best expenditures he makes are $20 books. He sees real value in the wisdom he gleans.

In this book, I am going to show you why you need to read, how to improve your reading, what you should be reading, where to find great reading material, and when to schedule this in your life. This is what I will be covering in *Read to Succeed*:

Why Reading Has Been Important to Me—I begin by highlighting the benefits I have received through reading. I share my interest in reading, the impact reading has had on my work and hobbies, and the effect podcasts have had on my reading.

Why You Must Read—Next, we will explore the research surrounding reading. You will learn about who reads, the gap between successful leaders and those just starting out, and the influence you can receive from experts who write books.

Famous People Who Found Reading Essential—Earlier, I dropped a few names of leaders who developed a strong reading habit. In this chapter you will learn about others who were avid readers and became successful, with examples from our Founding Fathers, political leaders, military leaders, and business leaders.

Benefits of Reading—Research has shown that reading can improve your health, put more money in your pocket, lead you to be more creative, improve your mental acuity, make you a better writer, and provide cheap entertainment.

Developing a Reading Habit—In this chapter, I will share ways to establish a reading goal, track your progress, and successfully complete your reading goal. To meet your reading goal, you will learn the importance of involving others in your reading pursuits. You will also learn how to find more time to read.

Reading Skills—There are techniques you can use to increase the number of books you read in a year if you have a desire to read more. You will be to able read more in the same period of time by increasing your vocabulary and using speed-reading techniques.

How to Read a Book—There are different ways to read. You can read simply for pleasure or read for increased knowledge. This chapter shares strategies for reading to increase knowledge. It will show you how to prepare for a reading session as well as how to read a book in an analytical manner.

Note-Taking—Note-taking is an important strategy if you want to make sense of what you are reading and benefit from the lessons in years to come. A number of note-taking techniques will be explored.

Reading Strategies—In this chapter, I outline two strategies that have helped me in life: Seek-Sense-Share and Invest-Learn-Teach.

What to Read—When deciding what to read, you must also decide how you will read it. In this chapter, I look at printed books, digital books, and audiobooks. Each book type has its pros and cons. Additionally, I share strategies for finding content to read so that you always have something on hand.

Reading and the Organization—Reading is not a solo activity. Businesses can help shape their culture by actively encouraging reading in their organization. In this chapter, we look at techniques you can employ to make this a success.

Build a Personal Library—Some of the most famous people in history had massive personal libraries. You will need to think about your library if you start to purchase books. This chapter provides you with strategies to think about as you create yours.

Doing Something with What You Read—This final chapter focuses on putting into practice what you have learned while reading. While you can become an expert based on what you learn while reading, the true benefits will occur when you start to implement the ideas and concepts you have learned about. You can also take it to the next level when you share what you learn with others.

Why should you listen to me? Throughout my life, I have always enjoyed reading. But it was when I started to read to solve problems that I realized the true power of reading. When I started to read with a purpose, I began to experience the benefits of reading. An organized reading habit helped me succeed at work, while volunteering, and during leisure activities. By learning through reading, I was able to improve more rapidly in all these activities. Reading allowed me to generate ideas at a faster and more consistent rate.

If you implement the strategies shared in this book, you will more than double your annual reading goals. If you are not currently an avid reader but want to be, you can easily start reading as many as fifty books each year. You will also discover that the more you read, the more ideas you will generate. If you put these ideas into practice, you will discover efficiencies and improved processes, which will lead to a better life.

Well, it's time to dig in. Let's start by exploring why you need to start a regular reading habit.

CHAPTER ONE

Why Reading Has Been Important to Me

"Man's flight through life is sustained by the power of his knowledge."
—AUSTIN "DUSTY" MILLER, on the *Eagle and Fledgling* statue at the
U.S. Air Force Academy

"No man's education is ever finished. A man's reading program should
be as carefully planned as his daily diet, for that too is food, without
which he cannot mentally develop." —NAPOLEON HILL

The two quotes above epitomize my ideas of learning and reading. A
regular reading habit has supported my lifelong journey of professional
improvement. I loved reading as a kid, and I appreciate it more as an
adult. Reading as a youth helped shape me into the person I am today.

My Interest in Reading

When I talk with faculty at colleges and universities, I find myself
hearing the same thing over and over—too often students do not want
to read or are not reading effectively. I could not understand this, because books have helped me achieve so many things, and some of these
books surround me even now as I write. I listen to podcasts of highly
successful people as I travel to and from work. Each highlights the importance of reading, and many of the books I read come from their
recommendations.

When I compare those struggling students to entrepreneurs on top of the world, I conclude that the success of many of the entrepreneurs springs from an attitude of continuous learning. What they read and how much they read was a large part of their learning. Thus, an idea was born to discuss what has become a natural part of my life—read to succeed.

This book's focus is reading to benefit one's profession. There is no end to what can be learned by benefiting from the writing of others. Developing a regular reading routine will feed you with a steady stream of ideas, as well as expanding your knowledge base in an informal learning program, whether that is professional or personal.

Before I dive into this idea of professional reading, I want to describe my own reading journey.

Reading as a Child

I loved to read as a young boy. I was a regular fixture at the Tunkhannock Public Library in Pennsylvania. I remember walking a couple of blocks to the library, a Queen Anne–style, two-story, red-brick building. As I walked up the steps and pushed open the heavy door, I entered a magical place. The collections were on large wooden shelves just to the left as one walked through the entrance. At least once a week, I would check out mysteries: adventures such as the Hardy Boys or Dick Prescott Goes to West Point series, and magic books. I am in good company—President Obama also enjoyed reading the Hardy Boys.[1] I would walk into the library and check out my quota of books, returning a week later to do it again. I can still smell the musty scent from all those old books if I close my eyes. I would try to go to the school library as much as possible in middle school and high school. All the great things I could learn fascinated me.

Reading While in the Air Force

My level of reading and enthusiasm tapered off once I left high school. After high school, I joined the Air Force. When I attended the United States Air Force Academy Preparatory School, I began to read more as part of my academics. I do not remember spending much time in base libraries. I do remember buying magazines, however. Because I was gung-ho then, they were often *Soldier of Fortune* magazines. I would also buy an occasional war story. This continued throughout my Air Force career, and I rekindled my interest in history, specifically military history. I can't say that all the reading was fun, but it was like relighting a pilot light. I was beginning to understand and appreciate the importance of reading at the professional level.

Reading to Be an Instructional Technologist

I had earned a master's degree in instructional technology by the time I left the Air Force. I landed a job at a small liberal arts college to manage instructional technology for a modern languages department. As the only instructional technologist on campus, my assignment was to set up a Mac lab to support the modern languages department, which included French, Spanish, Chinese, Japanese, Russian, Greek, and Latin. The problem was, I was not fluent with Macs, the foreign languages, or the programming languages I would need to make this happen. A Linux server was also part of the package.

I immediately invested in a stack of books to help me close the knowledge gap. I hoped to get the lab up and running over the summer, in time for the fall school term. This would not be the only time I would rush to buy a stack of books to help me fill a knowledge void.

After a couple of years as the instructional technologist, my role was expanded to campus webmaster. While I knew quite a bit about creating static web pages, it was time to broaden my knowledge and learn how to create dynamic web pages.

Reading to Learn to Be a Webmaster

The system I inherited ran on a language called Active Server Pages (ASP). ASP was dynamic web scripting and was a change from the basic HTML pages I was running. I looked forward to the new places I could take the website with this language. As with most new learning ventures, my learning curve was initially steep. Most of my advancements in this area evolved from reading books on ASP and ASP server management, as well as conducting specific searches on the web. I was trying to accomplish a specific task in most cases. I had to find out if ASP could handle the problem and, if so, how. Most challenges I faced came from the creative minds of the campus communications department responsible for the look and content of the campus website. Undoubtedly, the reading I did was critical to the success of the project.

Shortly after taking over as webmaster, I grasped the importance of creating dynamic websites using a language like ASP and supporting them with a database. With each problem solved, there arose new advances and challenges to tackle. The solutions were augmented by the extensive reading I did using a variety of sources.

One challenge involved using structured query language (SQL) for managing data. My learning curve with database management mirrored that of learning ASP, except I had a jump start on SQL because of a course I had taken for my master's degree. I was not happy about the course at the time, but in hindsight, the class was one of the most important courses I had taken.

During my time at the small liberal arts college, I would pore over books to gain insight into how things should operate, and used the books as references as I worked on specific problems. I became skilled at conducting Google searches as part of my problem-solving strategy. During this time, I realized there were people in online communities who were eager to assist. I became a regular in many of these communities as I sought help. Over time, I would offer them help in turn. Finally, I would bounce ideas off colleagues. In most cases, they were more than happy to assist, but only if I had exhausted my other resources. Most important, everything I learned and shared was first supported by professional reading.

In the end, I built a content management system for the campus website. What I learned and designed helped me gain a new job as a webmaster, this time at a university.

Reading to Support Cooperative Extension

After some time, I returned to work as an instructional technologist. This time I worked with the University of Wyoming Extension Service. This was a fascinating group to work with. The subject matter experts were quite diverse. They supported their communities in many areas, including nutrition, community planning, sustainable agriculture, and range management. Not only were they learning to be educators in each of their counties; they were also learning how to use technology to support instruction.

I was pursuing my doctorate while I was working with them. My love for reading went into overdrive, in large part due to the degree program, of which reading was an extensive component. My program focused on informal learning as it related to the professional development of extension educators. I learned about the place professional reading played in their ongoing development. Professional reading was one of the methods extension educators used to stay current in their subject matter expertise and, to a lesser degree, to become better educators.[2] Curiously, they did not rely on professional reading to strengthen their knowledge of technology, a fact that remains puzzling to me. Through my study, I also discovered their level of education affected how much they read. "Educators with a master's degree or higher rated professional reading significantly higher than those with less than a master's degree."[3] Additionally, the Gen Xers relied upon professional reading more than other age groups.

I began to attend professional conferences while working with cooperative extension. I attended the Association for Talent Development conference each year. I met thought leaders in learning and development and heard about books they had written. At each conference, I would leave with about $500 worth of books that would fuel my professional development as an educator for the next year.

Reading in Graduate School

My enthusiasm for reading was not rekindled until a recent graduate program. Not only was I reading a lot because of the classes I was taking, I was also doing a lot of reading to support my work. The more I read, the more ideas I generated for work and school. The value of a regular reading program was becoming clearer. In my dissertation, I wrote:

> Reading the works of Dewey, Knowles, Lindeman, Cross, Garrison, Marsick and Watkins, and Tough have been most educational. These authors have resonated with me and have helped me clarify my position on learning, education, and teaching. I believe learning is a lifelong process. Learning can be formal or informal, but it must be the responsibility of the learner. While each type of learning is necessary, I

have found informal learning to be most beneficial to my day-to-day life. It is the learning mode that I use the most. I am currently trying to understand how to informally learn in a more efficient manner.[4]

Reading to Support a Community College

Three years ago, I started to work as the technology-enhanced-instruction director at a community college. As I assumed the position, which included responsibility for two employees, I relied on the managerial training I received in the Air Force. This knowledge has served me well. When I arrived, my team was not able to get tasks completed in the time allotted, even though they were extremely knowledgeable. The systems and processes were not getting the hoped-for results. My team and I worked hard the first year to establish systems to move from a reactive to proactive system. To make this transformation, I read many books to identify the elements I wanted to put into place for our team.

Lifelong Reading

Professional reading has been the centerpiece of my informal learning. Not only have I increased the amount of reading; I have also changed how I read. I am now doing more reading on my Kindle device. I have also started to take notes on everything I read. With my Kindle, I highlight my notes and later transfer them into Zotero, a citation-management tool, where I use the notes to support my writing. My notes go into Zotero if I am reading something on a professional level.

At one time, I wanted nothing to do with school. I couldn't wait to graduate from high school and join the Air Force. But a fire to learn was lit while at the Air Force Academy Prep School. Thirty-one years later, I finished a terminal degree program. However, that was only a start. I am now doing more reading, writing, and learning than ever. I am excited about the idea of learning, and reading is a central component.

Reading to Support My Hobbies

Reading has also been important to my time away from work. Two of my many activities have been lifelong pursuits: magic and martial arts.

Magic

I have loved magic since I was a little boy. I dabble in it on a very amateur level, yet I love to read about and watch it. I have amassed a rather extensive library of magic books and videos. I also subscribe to a magic journal called *The Linking Rings*. I would study various techniques and strategies as I would any academic or professional topic.

Martial Arts

Another activity I have pursued for thirty years has also had a significant impact on my views of learning. The pursuit is a martial art: Bujinkan Budo Taijutsu, or Bujinkan for short. The Bujinkan is a martial art under the direction of Soke Masaaki Hatsumi. There are dojos, or schools, around the world, and I have led one since 1988. My involvement with this martial art began in North Dakota, where I happened to come upon a book I thought interesting. This led me to explore the possibilities of training in this martial art. While perusing a book stand for martial arts magazines, I found an address to an organization called the Shadows of Iga. With no group to train with, I attempted to learn based on what I was reading from the magazines and books. I also read the *Shadows of Iga* monthly newsletter.

When I moved to Turkey, I was still reading about Bujinkan and attempting to apply what I was reading. I met another practitioner approximately midway through my assignment. We became inseparable for the rest of my tour and trained together several times a week. He worked to correct my mistakes. We started purchasing videotapes and books to advance our training. We would review and practice what we had seen on video and read in the books. With his assistance, my personal training improved.

I had an opportunity to train with many wonderful instructors through the years. Books, magazines, and newsletters would support my training.

The Effect of Podcasts on My Reading

Listening to podcasts has shaped my mindset toward continuous learning. They reference great books that have helped entrepreneurs on their paths to success. I have followed their lead and started to read these books. What I learned I have applied to my work and volunteering. The effects have been notable, and the information I acquired has helped me to be more efficient and effective.

I discovered during my journey that I love to learn. Informal learning has shaped me and has fueled my love of learning. Learning thought leader Harold Jarche gave a name to what I loved doing—Seek-Sense-Share.

Wrap Up

I cannot imagine a life without books. I enjoyed reading as a child. Although I lapsed through high school, my habit of reading was rejuvenated during my time at the United States Air Force Academy Preparatory School. New challenges and problem solving required professional reading. Reading has helped me move through academic systems to eventually my doctorate. Reading and communicating with colleagues through various venues are integral parts of my progress in tackling new and interesting projects. My personal hobbies are enhanced with a reading program. As a result of my experiences, I have become a lifelong learner, and much of that learning is achieved through reading.

It has probably become obvious that I am extremely enthusiastic about reading and feel it has had a profound impact on my life. In the next chapter, you will discover reasons why you should also develop a professional reading habit.

CHAPTER TWO

Why You Must Read

"The man who does not read has no advantage over the man who cannot read." —MARK TWAIN

In chapter one, you saw the passion I have for reading. Not only do I always have a book in my hand; I have also discussed reading in numerous blog posts. The subject has been on my radar so much, I am now seeing and hearing about reading in articles and podcasts I frequent.

Research has demonstrated that students who don't read proficiently at the end of third grade are four times more likely to not finish high school.[5] Being literate helps you learn countless other subjects. You are at the mercy of others if you're illiterate.

I wrote this book because I recognized a disparity between how much most college students read as compared to successful business leaders. I hear professors say students are no longer reading. On the other hand, I read about and listen to podcasts highlighting how successful leaders are devouring books to learn as much as they possibly can. I want to encourage others to read more. A healthy reading habit should be part of your routine if you wish to be successful.

What You Need to Know

"Reading maketh a full man; conference a ready man; and writing an exact man." —Francis Bacon

There is a secret out there that successful leaders are sharing, but few are listening to—reading can help one become more successful! The rich and affluent devote a considerable number of hours to reading and self-improvement compared to other segments of society. This chapter explores the importance of reading for professional development. We will examine who is reading, focusing on a gap between reluctant student readers and successful leaders. Finally, we will see how reading can help you build your own team of coaches.

Books Are Essential Tools

Books are idea containers.[6] Books have attributes that make them powerful tools for learning: They are easily available, cheap, quickly absorbed, and current.[7] Purchasing a book at a store or online, or checking one out from a library, is very easy. You can become competent on a topic in mere hours and stay current on information.

I may do a cursory look on the internet if I am approaching a new topic. However, if I need to pursue a topic in depth, I have found investing in a book is worth my time. As Ralph Besse says, "Books present the finest of all reading opportunities. The greatest thinking of the finest minds, the finest expression of the greatest writers and the most profound learning of qualified experts in every field and every age is available in books."[8]

Reading Is Central to Business Success

I did not grasp how important professional reading was until I read David Cottrell's book, *Tuesday Morning Coaching*. One of his statements surprised me: "According to the U.S. Labor Department, business people who read at least seven business books per year earn over 230 percent more than people who read just one book per year."[9]

This makes a lot of sense. People who want to be and stay successful are always learning. Reading is a great way to tap into new ideas, regardless of one's discipline. Books provide a long, deep conversation with another thinker.[10] As Postolovski notes, the ideas from a book stay with an individual a lot longer than a blog post, thus the benefits are greater. This is primarily because reading a book is a deep dive into a subject, whereas blog posts are shallow glimpses into one aspect of a topic.

While I was poking around on the internet, I learned that 20 to 25 percent of Americans have not read a book in the past year.[11] However, many sources note that CEOs are reading four to six books per month. Leaders like Bill Gates and President Obama take vacations for reading and reflecting. This speaks volumes about the power and necessity of reading for professional development.

Reading is one of the most important skills to learn. Being literate will help you learn countless other subjects. Mark Twain's quote at the beginning of the chapter resonates today because the fact remains that you are at the mercy of others if you don't read.

Who Reads?

According to the Pew Research Center, 76 percent of adults read a book in 2013.[12] There are about three times the number of nonreaders today, compared to 1978.[13] Yet there is an increase in reading for younger adults (ages eighteen to twenty-nine), and they were most likely to read.[14] Millennials make up 37 percent of the book-buying market.[15] This group is investing in printed books. Additionally, women were more likely to read a book than men.[16] Those with some college education or a college degree were more likely to read compared to a high school graduate or less. Finally, those making more than $50,000 a year were the most likely to read a book.

When it comes to e-books, women also outpace men by 10 percentage points.[17] Additionally, eighteen- to twenty-nine-year-olds are more likely to consume an e-book, as are college graduates. Furthermore, those who make $75,000 or more and those who live in urban or suburban communities consumed at least one e-book in 2013.

Why Do People Read?

According to adults, reading is the most important skill to learn next to communications.[18] According to a survey conducted by the PEW Research Center, Americans read for a variety of reasons: for pleasure (80 percent), keeping up with current events (78 percent), research on a specific topic (74 percent), and to stay current for work or school (56 percent).[19]

The adults surveyed cited various reasons when asked why they liked reading: learning and gaining knowledge, escaping reality and using their imagination, enjoying a good story and plot, and relaxing.[20] Two percent of those asked noted they liked the physical properties of books. Affluent members of our society read to increase their knowledge of a topic to make more money or to help clients make more money, learn how to become more successful, stay abreast of current events, develop their mind, and learn new things.[21] According to the PEW study, "In overall reading habits, heavy readers in urban and suburban communities are involved in reading for the acquisition of information and knowledge more so than heavy readers in rural areas."[22]

How Much Is Read?

American adults read an average of twelve books in 2013.[23] Women read more than men. Those between thirty and sixty-four read more than other age groups. Those with a post-secondary education read more than high school graduates or less, with college graduates reading the most. Individuals earning $50,000 or more and those living in rural communities read the most. Thirty-two percent of readers are light readers, those reading one to five books during the past year; 29 percent of readers are moderate readers, reading six to twenty books per year; and 18 percent are heavy readers, reading over twenty-one books per year.[24] Twenty percent of the population did not read a book in the past year. Those who live in a rural area stood out compared to their urban and suburban counterparts—26 percent of those living in a rural community had not read a book in the past year. Since 1992, the number of people who read for pleasure has been steadily declining.[25]

What does this research tell us? Those who are better educated and making $50,000 or more a year are reading more. Is this because they can devote more time and money to reading? That is undetermined. Perhaps it is because they recognize the importance of reading as it relates to their success.

ssions I have had lately with faculty have been about ⅃ing. Have students not yet grasped the importance of ⅂tands in contrast to the many successful leaders who have useᒑ ⅃ing to propel their learning forward once they left formal education.[26] I have since understood the importance of reading as related to success. But I have to admit there was a time when I did not read much. The graduate program at the University of Wyoming rekindled my interest.

Students Do Not Want to Read

There is a perception from faculty and librarians that students do not like to read, at least as it relates to school.[27] However, while librarians are not seeing a lot of recreational reading, faculty members do report that students are reading for entertainment when they have time.

Unfortunately, there are many who do not see the importance of reading and continual learning. "Mark Bauerlein, in his book, *The Dumbest Generation,* reveals how a whole generation of youth is being dumbed down by their aversion to reading anything of substance and their addiction to digital 'crap' via social media."[28] In 2009, the National Assessment of Educational Progress reported that approximately 50 percent of students read well enough to attend college. They simply do not *want* to read. There is a term for this: aliteracy. According to a 2004 National Endowment for the Arts report, there has been a decline in daily reading and overall reading despite an increased ranking in literacy.[29] Note that Facebook first came on the scene in 2004 as a program for Harvard students. In 2004, social media had not yet become mainstream, although the internet had been mainstream for about ten years. During this time, approximately 50 percent of students were still reading books for recreational reasons; this is in comparison to a 1991 study, which found 88 percent of students reported reading for pleasure.[30] "Far too many students complete their assigned readings and duly receive their grades and degrees, but they emerge from their educational experiences with their distaste for and avoidance of reading relatively untouched."[31] Fewer and fewer college students continue to read after graduating.

While in college, students are not reading except to support a class, if that. A U.S. Public Interest Group survey reported that approximately 70 percent of students did not buy a textbook due to cost at least once in their college career.[32] In another study, 77 percent of students surveyed indicated they had already done enough reading for class.[33] They did not believe extra reading was worth their time.

In 2011, a study examined whether students were using technology such as e-readers to support their reading.[34] Out of the 1,705 respondents, only 23.5 percent read e-books, and the majority who did not read e-books did not plan to own an e-reading device. Prices for the device and e-books, along with selection, were significant factors in their decision.

Students Struggle with Reading

A college student's success relates to their reading success. There is a significant amount of reading in the typical college curriculum and even more reading associated with the elite schools. Students who struggle with reading and have weak vocabularies will comment that reading is one of the most challenging parts of a college education.[35]

College success is thus tied to improving reading skills such as reading speed and vocabulary. One of the key strategies to increase vocabulary is to read more, even if it is recreational.

Students who are ideal readers are better students; an ideal reader is one who is engaged and avidly reads. They tend to get better grades, think more critically, and have higher levels of comprehension. Additionally, motivated readers have higher levels of achievement. However, in a 2014 study, 53 percent of the students surveyed self-reported they were unenthusiastic readers.[36] This is down from a 2011 study, in which 93 percent of students had read for pleasure.[37] Yet in the 2014 study, when students were approached with reading as an intellectual challenge, the result showed 83 percent of students indicated they were enthusiastic about reading.[38]

One of the problems with reading in college compared to self-directed reading is that instructors in college direct the choice of the book. "For every student who loved the books that teachers selected, it seemed we had another who resented the fact that the reading was assigned and students had no choice in the matter."[39] Students are not fans of boring books. When students believe reading is an obligation, only 19 percent are enthusiastic. It is all about choice. In many schools, there is a significant disconnect between what students want to read and archaic literature the instructor teaches.[40] If reading is an important skill to learn, schools must consider what students want to read and create a balance. Educators must tap into the excitement of reading. It is the difference between "want to" and "have to." Self-directed readers choose what to read and when. Many students become frustrated with reading because they "have to," whereas successful leaders read because they "want to." Studies has shown that if instructors recommended books to read rather than required them, students had more enthusiasm for reading.[41]

A student's major also affects reading enthusiasm. Those in the humanities read more and have more enthusiasm for reading than those in majors like sciences, health sciences, and mathematics.[42] Internet use has also had a negative effect on reading.[43] According to a 2014 study, students spend more time reading on the internet than they do for reading for academic or extracurricular purposes.[44]

Introducing learners to content they may not come across in their self-directed approach to selecting reading content is one of the purposes of higher education. Are colleges beginning to make it too easy for learners? Are colleges taking the challenge out of reading assignments? As Thorne says: "The adapt-to-the-students-you-actually-have mantra prevails. Selection committees match the book to the abilities of the least capable students. More-capable students frequently complain that the books are insultingly clichéd and immature."[45]

When selecting books as part of the common summer reading program, do not shy away from challenging and stimulating books. Keep the selection committee small, use top novel and nonfiction reading lists as a guide, develop an intellectual culture that encourages charting new learning paths, and continue to raise the bar.

Instructors and coordinators should consider a move to e-books. Students recognize the value of e-books and e-readers, but they avoid using them because of price and selection.[46] If a campus made an investment in e-readers with a pre-populated collection of books, this could be a way to improve reading on campus.

Campus libraries should also be looking for ways to strengthen their e-reading program.

Campus librarians can have a huge impact on student reading. Some academic librarians believe they should only support academic reading, but research shows all reading helps increase academic standing, and including reading for recreation is therefore a positive step. Librarians should put out recommended book lists, increase recreational books, develop more recreational-book displays, provide areas for leisure reading, offer incentives for reading, extend loan periods across holidays and summer, and highlight what fellow students are reading.[47] Librarians, with the help of faculty, should do what they do best—suggest reading material to interested students. Gilbert and Fister note:

> If we want our students to continue to read after college, we should look beyond helping them succeed as students, but also consider ways to help them develop their personal reading tastes, learn effective ways to identify satisfying reading material, and instill an expectation that they can turn to libraries after college for their continued education and development.[48]

Great Books

Some college students are seeking challenging reading opportunities. To this end, colleges across the nation are using the Great Books curriculum. This curriculum focuses on a collection of foundational books from Plato to Dickens and Jefferson to Locke, covering literature, philosophy, and science. Some of the more noteworthy books include *Meditations* by Marcus Aurelius, *On the Revolutions of Heavenly Spheres* by Nicolaus Copernicus, *The Origin of Species by Means of Natural Selection* by Charles Darwin, and *The Federalist* by Alexander Hamilton, James Madison, and John Jay. The curriculum is not easy. There are over 160 authors on the list, and over a hundred colleges are using the great books as part of their program. To read all 29 million words in the Great Books series would take an average reader around two thousand hours.[49] Finishing all the great books is on my bucket list.

Successful Leaders Read Voraciously

Reading is an effective way to advance personal and professional development. As Michael Hyatt notes in his article "Five Ways Reading Makes You a Better Leader," almost everyone who is a successful leader is also an avid reader.[50] Successful leaders know that reading provides ideas and direction. It also keeps them from making unnecessary mistakes.

"If you want to get ahead in business, sit down and pick up a book. Warren Buffett spends 80 percent of his day reading. Bill Gates reads for an hour each night before going to bed. Also, Mark Cuban credits part of his success to the fact that he is willing to read more than anyone else."[51]

Professionals like Buffett, Gates, and Cuban take part in informal learning and professional development. They are networking with others, reading literature, and attend learning opportunities.

Successful leaders focus on continual improvement. A regular reading habit is one of the key methods for their self-improvement. Over 80 percent of the affluent members of our society love to read, read two or more books per month, and read thirty or more minutes per day.[52] The wealthy will read two or more self-improvement books per month. This is in stark contrast to the poorer sections of our society. The majority of the poor do not love to read, as demonstrated by the fact that only 15 percent will read two or more books per month, and only 2 percent read thirty or more minutes each day. The average American reads only nineteen minutes per day.[53] There is also a sharp contrast between the activities of the wealthy and the poor. For example, approximately 70 percent of the wealthy watch TV for less than sixty minutes per day, compared to 23 percent of poor people.[54] Furthermore, wealthy people tend not to engage in watching reality TV shows. Successful people use their time on self-improvement rather than entertainment.

Successful leaders are reading books that will challenge their business outlook.[55] However, they are not only reading books to improve their skills and business acumen; they also read blogs, newspapers, magazines, and newsletters.[56]

"There are many examples of successful people dropping out of school or foregoing a formal education, but it is clear that they never stop learning, and reading is a key part of their success."[57]

In a podcast interview, John Lee Dumas, entrepreneur and host of the podcast *Entrepreneurs on Fire*, discussed the importance of reading with successful musician and entrepreneur Gene Simmons. Simmons indicated reading was the most important skill to develop. It was the path to success. He talked about the importance of the Gutenberg Press because it made reading available to the masses.[58] Before the printing press, only the literate and elite could read; it was a way to control the class system. If one wants to have an equal footing, he or she needs to read.

Stand on the Shoulders of Giants

The power of reading is learning from the successes and mistakes of others. Why spend unnecessary energy and time trying to learn a lesson the hard way, when others who have already learned the lesson are willing to pass it on to you? In the interview, Simmons said: "Reading about historic business, military, social and political leaders from the US and across the world gives you a window into the past, and a better perspective on how historic leaders have shaped the world we live in now, and will live in the future."[59]

There is much to learn from leaders who shaped history. These lessons can help us be more effective and efficient wherever we are.

Reading can have a transforming effect. The information and knowledge we gain through reading can help us form new ideas and lead to breakthroughs in our careers. It can also open up proven methods of success.

I have a twenty-five-minute commute to work each day. This gives me almost an hour that I can devote to learning. My learning tool of choice for these situations has been the podcast. One podcast I have found particularly helpful is the aforementioned *Entrepreneurs on Fire*. During this podcast, Dumas interviews a different successful entrepreneur each day. While there are many lessons, there are many themes that seem to shine through. One topic interviewees have emphasized over and over is the importance of coaches and mentors to the learning process. While I would love one-on-one mentoring on many topics, it can be cost prohibitive or difficult to arrange the opportunities. But I do have access to countless coaches on many subjects, and so does everyone else.

CEOs, celebrities, and professional athletes take advantage of coaches and mentors to help them improve their performances. Coaches and mentors are not only for the rich and famous—everyone can stand on the shoulders of giants. In *Start: Punch Fear in the Face, Escape Average, Do Work That Matters*, Jonathan Acuff comments on the positive effects working with others have on the learning process.[60]

A significant advantage of reading is that an individual can benefit from the coaching and mentoring of countless people who have learned valuable lessons and want to share them. In other words, you can add a group of mentors to your team through the power of reading. Nearly 75 percent of successful business leaders reported they self-mentor by reading and experimenting.[61] Individuals can only achieve so much in their tiny bubbles. But they can expand that bubble by bringing in the ideas of others through reading. We often think our problems are unique, but there is a great chance others have faced the same type of problem, and that they have written a solution to the problem.[62]

"And yet reading—especially, I would argue, reading books—remains one of the most important paths to real knowledge."[63] It is important to invest in professional development. Reading is a key component of that development. You should consider spending 3 percent of your earnings on personal development by purchasing books and magazines, online and face-to-face training, and audio and video training.[64] Fortunately, you can find a lot of great training materials online for free.

With each book I read, I try to write a quick book review to reflect upon what I read. I often pull one or two new ideas into my practices. My new team hates Mondays because I often come in with lots of new ideas. But they are finding that not all of them are bad!

Wrap Up

Business leaders and entrepreneurs extol the importance of reading in their professional development. They have made reading a priority in their lives and the results speak for themselves. Yet many Americans are held back because they do not share this same interest in reading. College students demonstrate an increasing lack of interest in reading beyond minimum requirements for individual courses. Reading offers a cost-effective way to take advantage of being mentored by someone with expertise. Even those on the poorest level of society can receive the coaching of others if they read. Reading saves time in avoiding making mistakes by reading about other people's experiences and solutions.

The next chapter highlights leaders who have achieved greatness in large part because of their reading habits. These leaders come from all walks of life, including politics, business, and entertainment.

CHAPTER THREE

Famous People Who Found Reading Essential

"A readership crisis is really a leadership crisis." —MICHAEL HYATT

In chapter two, you read about reasons why you should take up reading. Reading is a powerful tool for success. Reading has not only been essential to my career, but has also helped fuel some of the organizations I have been part of. I am not the only person reading has shaped. Many political, business, and military leaders rely upon reading to shape their ideas. All have different approaches to their reading, why they read, and how they have benefited.

Let's begin with our Founding Fathers.

Our Founding Fathers Valued Reading

Our Founding Fathers, as they were shaping our nation, reached back to the knowledge they had gained through extensive reading. They had a deep interest in history and used their knowledge to write the founding documents of our nation.[65] The volume of information consumed and created by leaders like Thomas Jefferson, John Adams, and Benjamin Franklin is astounding. Jefferson would sometimes read ten or twelve hours per day.[66]

Reading was central to their lives. Our Founding Fathers used books as tools to improve what they were doing at the time: running businesses, governing, being lawyers, farming their fields, or creating new inventions. Books were a primary source of knowledge as they advanced their crafts. They took pride in being able to hold intelligent arguments, a product of their classical training.

Adams and Jefferson, as well as many other Founding Fathers, could read and write Greek and Latin. They read original texts in the native languages; they had to be proficient in Greek and Latin as a prerequisite to going to college.[67] They would take notes in these different languages. They also wrote Latin and Greek phrases in letters and documents they sent to colleagues. "Jefferson used so many Greek quotes in his letters to Adams (who liked Latin better than Greek) that, on one occasion, Adams complained to him about it."[68] Our Founding Fathers relied upon these ancient texts to help develop a new government. "Not only are the Federalist Papers replete with classical references, but the pseudonyms each of the writers chose for themselves were all taken from the writers of classical times."[69]

Their love for reading came at a financial cost. They all created their own libraries. "Unfortunately, books were quite expensive in the Colonies—in 1776, a first edition of Adam Smith's 'The Wealth of Nations' would have cost about $615 in today's dollars, about the same as an iPad costs today."[70] One can recognize how important professional reading was to our Founding Fathers.

President Thomas Jefferson

The third president, Thomas Jefferson, was a prolific reader and writer. He owned between nine and ten thousand books during his life.[71] He spent hours each day reading nonfiction books on subjects such as agriculture, science, history, philosophy, law, and literature. "Jefferson was fascinated with languages and philology (study of literary texts and written records). He read in seven languages—English, Greek, Latin, French, Italian, Spanish, and Anglo-Saxon. He collected Indian vocabularies and owned dictionaries and grammars in languages such as Arabic, Welsh, and Gaelic."[72] He preferred reading texts in their original language rather than in translation, because he believed he received the proper meaning. "Jefferson relied on his books as his chief source of inspiration and practical knowledge, and believed that education was the means to an enlightened and informed citizenry that would help preserve democracy."[73] Jefferson had little regard for fiction. In a letter to Nathaniel Burwell in 1818, Jefferson wrote that he felt reading fiction was a waste of time, except for stories based on real-life events through which lessons could be learned.

Jefferson received a liberal arts education.[74] He learned Latin, Greek, and French as well as literature, poetry, history, mathematics, and geography. He read what are now considered the great books of Western civilization. Jefferson went to the College of William and Mary, where he continued to develop his liberal arts studies. He then apprenticed as a lawyer, during which time he studied English common law through rigorous reading.

Jefferson developed his mindset for national governance through extensive reading. He was a disciplined reader who read with a purpose.[75] He kept a detailed list of books he owned, a list of books he wanted to read, and a reading schedule. Jefferson maintained many commonplace books (notebooks) to track his political affairs as well as record observations from his readings.[76]

Jefferson was on the lookout for new books to buy everywhere he went.[77] He was a frequent visitor to Paris bookstores, collecting books on science and the Americas; he added to his debt because of his love of books. Jefferson kept a meticulous collection. He arranged his books in three distinct areas: history, philosophy, and fine arts.[78] He arranged each section into smaller sections. Jefferson built his physical library on a couple of occasions. He had to rebuild his initial library. In one case, he lost books due to a fire. He also used his personal collection to help start the Library of Congress. Because of his vast library, when requested, he created a book list for the second generation of Library of Congress and later for the University of Virginia. He did more for the Library of Congress than create a book list. In 1815, Jefferson donated over 6,500 books to replace 3,000 books destroyed in a fire when the British burned the capital.[79]

Books were the cornerstone of his life. He constantly built upon his knowledge through his reading habit and maintained an extensive library to reference throughout his life.

Lessons Learned from Thomas Jefferson

- Build a library you or your team can reference.
- Take time to read the classics.
- Broaden your view of the world.

Benjamin Franklin

One of the more colorful figures in U.S. history is Benjamin Franklin—diplomat, inventor, scientist, and writer. He was also a signer of three critical U.S. documents: the Declaration of Independence, the Treaty of Paris, and the United States Constitution. According to the *Autobiography of Benjamin Franklin*, Franklin learned to read as an adolescent.[80] He worked at being a scholar, while his older brothers pursued trade apprenticeships. Because of that potential as a scholar, his father transferred him from a grammar school to a school for writing and arithmetic. Though he was proficient in writing, he failed mathematics, and the school sent him home.

Franklin reports a great fondness for reading. When he had money, he would spend it on books.[81] As a boy, he wished he could find suitable books to read and became a printer's apprentice. He worked in an indentured status for his brother from the age of twelve until twenty-one. This afforded him the opportunity to read a wide array of books. He also borrowed books from booksellers in the evenings. He spent all night reading to get them back first thing in the morning.

As Franklin grew older, he became friends with some of the most avid readers in Boston.[82] They would read the same books and spend long nights discussing them. Throughout the *Autobiography of Benjamin Franklin*, Franklin would comment on the various people with whom he was friends and note their fondness of reading.

Later in life, Franklin would expand these late-night discussions. He created a learning club, called the Junto, which lasted forty years.[83]

We met on Friday evenings. The rules that I drew up required that every member, in his turn, should produce one or more queries on any point of Morals, Politics, or Natural Philosophy, to be discuss'd by the company; and once in three months produce and read an essay of his own writing, on any subject he pleased. Our debates were to be under the direction of a president, and to be conducted in the sincere spirit of inquiry after truth, without fondness for dispute, or desire of victory; and, to prevent warmth, all expressions of positiveness in opinions, or direct contradiction, were after some time made contraband, and prohibited under small pecuniary penalties.[84]

Junto capped membership at twelve. This sounds a lot like the Mastermind groups I have heard about in podcasts and read about in Napoleon Hill's book, *Think and Grow Rich*.

Franklin was so passionate about reading and learning that he developed the public library system in Philadelphia.[85] The library began as a subscription service through which members would pay for an initial investment of books to the system and then pay an annual fee to increase the number of books. The library was open once per week for lending, with a fine for overdue books.

Franklin noted: "This library afforded me the means of improvement by constant study, for which I set apart an hour or two each day, and thus repair'd in some degree the loss of the learned education my father once intended for me. Reading was the only amusement I allow'd myself."[86]

Franklin's success was no accident; it was based on a systematic daily regimen.[87] He dedicated at least an hour or two to learning each day, and designated a significant part of his learning to reading.

Franklin was intensely curious about everything. To understand what he read, he would engage in conversation with other avid readers. I believe he took reading to another level when he created the public library system and Junto. He understood the importance of sharing what he was learning.

Lessons Learned from Benjamin Franklin

- Surround yourself with others who are also keen to learn as a way to expand your ideas.
- Schedule time to read each day.
- Build your own library or leverage a public or private library.

President John Adams

"The Science of Government it is my Duty to study, more than all other Studies Sciences: the Art of Legislation and Administration and Negotiation, ought to take Place, indeed to exclude in a manner all other Arts. I must study Politicks and War that my sons may have liberty to study Painting and Poetry Mathematicks and Philosophy. My sons ought to study Mathematicks and Philosophy, Geography, natural History, Naval Architecture, navigation, Commerce and Agriculture, in order to give their Children a right to study Painting, Poetry, Musick, Architecture, Statuary, Tapestry and Porcelaine."[88]

John Adams, who wrote the above, was our second president and a noteworthy statesman. He was also an avid reader. He amassed a library of more than 3,500 books over his life.[89] However, his collection started slowly.

He was not interested in reading and studying when young, but his father encouraged him with a little ditchdigging. Adams quickly discovered that learning Latin was easier than the ditchdigging his father assigned to him. John was the oldest son, and his father was grooming him to attend college.[90] Adams received a classical education, in which professors expected him to read the classics in their original languages.[91] Additionally, instructors expected him to translate the books written in Greek or Latin into English and translate the English back into Greek or Latin. "Such a rigorous study of antiquity prepared John for the entrance examination at Harvard College, which he took in 1751."[92] He received a classical education at Harvard, studying Greek, Latin, rhetoric, natural and moral philosophy, metaphysics, geography, and mathematics.

Over time, Adams developed a love for reading. Both John Adams and his wife, Abigail, shared their love of reading with their children.[93] He took notes in the margins using native languages. Adams's personal correspondence reflected his classical background.[94] He was also an ardent defender of a classical education, as exhibited in his debate with Benjamin Rush, a fellow member of the Continental Congress.

Adams's classical education also served as a foundation for his book collection. Adams read in many topics, including philosophy, history, law, politics, and poetry.[95] Even when he was young, he would read his books with a pen in hand to take notes in the margins. These notes would later help shape history. The notes also gave him an opportunity to provide commentary, often in displeasure. For example, Adams wrote under a pseudonym, "Humphrey Ploughjogger," to the *Boston Gazette* in opposition to the Stamp Act. "His books served as essential tools in his varied roles as student, lawyer, revolutionary, diplomat, president, and elder statesman."[96]

The reading of books "was not an end in itself: it was a means for self-improvement and public service."[97] For example, Adams used his knowledge to defend the British soldiers involved in the "Boston Massacre." Adams believed literacy was an essential skill of citizens.[98] Adams and many of the other Founding Fathers believed a good education was essential to the nation; it created better voters.[99] He wrote:

> I must judge for myself, but how can I judge, how can any man judge, unless his mind has been opened and enlarged by reading? A man who can read will find . . . rules and observations that will enlarge his range of thought and enable him the better to judge who has and who has not that integrity of heart and that compass of knowledge and understanding which form the statesman."[100]

Adams was proud of the library he had built and willed his library to the people of Massachusetts.[101] Many of the volumes he donated had his signature inscribed in the front cover of the books.

Lessons Learned from John Adams

- Surround yourself with tools (books) so you can work more easily.
- Capture notes in the margins of books you are reading as a way to converse with the author.

President George Washington

George Washington, the first president of the United States, read out of necessity.[102] Washington did not go to college, but he understood the importance of literacy.[103] He "used reading as a means to an end—he wanted to know how to farm better, how to lead an army, how to lead a country, how to conduct himself civilly."[104]

Washington was adept at putting whatever he read to use. He used books to prepare himself, and he also had officers under his command study key military texts to help prepare for battle. He realized one could learn firsthand from one's own experience or from the experiences of others. Reading allows a person to benefit from the latter. He was not a fast reader, but he also did not have to reread passages.[105] Washington "wanted to learn things he could use, and given a limited amount of time, focused his attention where it was most profitable to him."[106] Washington continued to read because university-educated men, who would sometimes point out his shortcomings, surrounded him.[107]

Washington did not have the vast libraries like Adams, Franklin, and Jefferson, but he was interested in reading everything he could.

His library of nine hundred volumes was more practical.[108] The library contained a mix of classical and modern authors as well as a vast collection of maps and charts, which served him in his duties as a surveyor.[109] He was also fond of reading books on agriculture.

Lessons Learned from George Washington

- Increase your position in life by continuously learning.
- Focus on an area of interest.

Political Leaders

Harold Evans, author of the *New York Times* article "White House Book Club," became interested in the reading habits of American presidents while exploring the reading habits of President Clinton.[110] He discovered that over half of the presidents have had a passion for reading. He also compared them to their historical ranking. The twenty-two bibliophiles outpaced the nonreaders in historical rankings.

I chose presidents as my political leaders to review. The presidency is a distinct position in which, as of this writing, only forty-five people have had the opportunity to sit in the seat. Each president had to teach himself how to do the job. The successful ones relied upon reading to fill knowledge gaps.

Presidents can bump a book to the bestseller list as quickly as Oprah.[111] When the public and reporters see the president reading a particular book, the book tends to show up on the bestseller list. When Theodore Roosevelt favored an author, the author's reputation rose.[112] John F. Kennedy had a positive effect on Ian Fleming's reputation and book sales. Ronald Reagan helped Tom Clancy's *The Hunt for Red October* rise on the bestseller list. Many books Bill Clinton read advanced on the list. Barack Obama has often caused a book to receive a bestseller bump.

What presidents read has an impact on their policy decision-making. Reading helps them form ideas for their policies as well as provide them information that helps them change their position.[113] The books presidents read give insight into the direction the president wants to take the country.[114] Depending upon the situation or meeting they were about to involve themselves with, they would investigate historical precedence.

President Barack Obama

President Barack Obama, the forty-fourth president of the United States, was a night owl.[115] He often retreated to his study at about 7 p.m. to read reports, watch sports, and read novels. The last thing he did in the evening, around midnight, was read a book for a half hour to an hour. President Obama enjoyed relaxing with a novel,[116] and said he developed a higher level of empathy while reading fiction.[117] Through fiction, he has learned a lot about relationships and dealing with people who are different.[118] He cautioned that people need to read outside their comfort zone, so they are not reinforcing their own narrative. However, President Obama stuck to liberal authors and Ronald Reagan followed and read conservative authors.[119]

Obama would often read books that helped him better understand a situation in which he was involved.[120] As he was preparing to enter office in 2009, he read *Team of Rivals: The Political Genius of Abraham Lincoln*; *Ghost Wars: The Secret History of the CIA, Afghanistan, and Bin Laden, from the Soviet Invasion to September 10, 2001*;

and *Common Wealth: Economics for a Crowded Planet.* He also read books on climate change, poverty, and civil unrest throughout his two terms.

"Obama, like Kennedy and Clinton before him, seems keenly aware of the power of books to shape public perceptions."[121] Obama or members of his team would often reference a book he was reading. This would generate interest across the world.

Lessons Learned from Barack Obama

- Reading more fiction will help you better empathize with others.
- You can influence others by what you are reading.

President George W. Bush

President George W. Bush was the forty-third president of the United States. What many people do not realize is that he was an active reader.[122] President Bush did not promote his love for reading. He kept his reading private to protect his "non-elite" status.[123] Yet, his closest friends knew he loved to read. According to Karl Rove, "Mr. Bush loves books, learns from them, and is intellectually engaged by them."[124] From 2006 to 2008, Bush and Rove set and competed on annual reading goals. At the end of 2006, Bush had reportedly read 95 books. During that three-year span, he read 186 books.[125] According to his wife, Laura, President Bush would read every evening while in bed.[126]

President Bush's reading list consisted of historical biographies from Abraham Lincoln to Andrew Carnegie as well as "prescriptive" books to find solutions to problems he was facing.[127] He developed his appreciation of history from teachers where he went to school.[128] He was interested in the decision-making process of those who went before him and would read books from authors who had both liberal and conservative leanings.[129] He also enjoyed reading fiction. Additionally, he read the Bible in its entirety every year.

In *Decision Points*, Bush mentions numerous books that influenced his thinking in the White House.[130] He read so he would not repeat what he believed to be mistakes in previous administrations.

If Bush liked a particular author, he would try to arrange a meeting with the author.[131] Theodore Roosevelt did the same.

Lessons Learned from George W. Bush

- Read to help prevent mistakes already made by others.
- Read widely to understand the perspectives of all sides.

President Bill Clinton

President Bill Clinton is one of the best-read presidents of our time.[132] The *New York Times* described him as "an omnivorous reader."[133] When getting ready to move into the White House, the Clintons had to have additional bookshelves added. It seems the Clintons added new bookshelves to each of the executive mansions they lived in.[134] At the governor's mansion, the Clinton library had 4,500 books displayed, with a dozen unopened boxes of books.[135]

Clinton would read four to five books per week.[136] He especially enjoyed thrillers, mysteries, and historical texts. Often, he was reading more than one book at the same time. Fluent in German, Clinton would also read books and magazines in German. He would try to read thirty minutes each day as well as during the weekends or on plane rides.[137] One year, he read three hundred books.[138]

Understanding the impact his position had on different groups, he would leave a book out for members of the press to see and write about.[139]

Lesson Learned from Bill Clinton

- Make reading a priority and find opportunities to read.

President John F. Kennedy

John F. Kennedy was the thirty-fifth president of the United States. To succeed in this role, Kennedy conducted intensive research. He would read as much as he could on a subject until he understood it. For example, in 1945, when Kennedy wanted to know more about labor, he had his father send him a crate of books on the subject, and he spent his evenings reading until the crate was empty.[140]

When he was young, Kennedy suffered from many maladies, including scarlet fever, digestive issues, and back pain.[141] Kennedy spent his time reading while recovering.[142] Kennedy often read books on serious history.[143] He read almost everything written by or on Winston Churchill. He also enjoyed spy novels, such as the James Bond series by Ian Fleming.

Kennedy understood the importance of having his team thinking in the same way. If he found a book applicable to his team, he would share it. For example, he shared *Guns of August* with military officers to educate them about mistakes that led to World War I.[144]

Kennedy could read 1,200 words a minute.[145] He learned how to read faster as a young man by using speed-reading techniques and taking a speed-reading course.[146] He worked on decreasing the number of fixations (where one's eyes come to rest when reading) and saccades (the "jump" one's eyes make when reading) by increasing the number of words seen in each fixation.[147] As president, he also encouraged his staff to learn how to be faster readers. He used speed-reading to his advantage as he read books, reports, and newspapers.[148] As part of his daily morning routine, he would read five newspapers and, according to an article in *Life* magazine, he would also read a couple of newspapers in the afternoon. When he traveled, he would pick up the local papers to read.[149] He would also pick up a myriad of magazines to feed his unstoppable appetite for information.

Lessons Learned from John F. Kennedy

- Learn to improve your reading speed and proficiency so you can consume more valuable information.
- Quickly come up to speed on a topic by carefully selecting a stack of books on the topic and read them.

President Franklin Roosevelt

Franklin D. Roosevelt was the thirty-second president of the United States. Roosevelt was well read and amassed a personal library of 22,000 volumes.[150] He had an affinity for naval history, political history, and biographies.[151] As Assistant Secretary of the Navy, he had collected 10,000 books about the Navy and read each one of them.[152] He also enjoyed fictional works by Kipling, Carroll, and Hawthorne, and the poetry of Longfellow and Tennyson. Additionally, he enjoyed detective stories.

Because of his physical disabilities, Roosevelt was often confined to a wheelchair, from which he would pursue his hobbies: stamp collecting and reading. He became highly proficient at reading, in part because he worked to develop his speed-reading capabilities.[153] He could read a paragraph at one glance, and sometimes a page at a glance.[154]

Lessons Learned from Franklin D. Roosevelt

- Build a library you can easily reference.
- Keep improving your reading speed and proficiency.

President Theodore Roosevelt

Theodore Roosevelt was the twenty-sixth president of the United States. He placed a high priority on reading to stay abreast of what was happening in the world. A fast reader, he would read one to three books per day.[155] According to research, he would read a book before breakfast. He also enjoyed time at the end of a day to relax with a book.[156] He enjoyed reading in a diverse range of genres. He read whatever happened to grab his attention, but he had a particular fondness for naval history and natural sciences.[157] He developed an expertise across a myriad of topics that served him in his various political offices. Roosevelt developed his love of reading at an early age. He suffered from asthma as a boy, and would take refuge in his bed with a book when he had an asthma attack.[158] This love for reading would stay with him throughout his life.

By his own account, Roosevelt read over 10,000 books.[159] He could do this because he skimmed and scanned his way through nonessential material. His comprehension was extremely high; he could concentrate fully at the task at hand and ignore all other distractions.[160] When he settled into a reading session, he gave it his full attention. Not all the books were written in English.

He would always have a book with him and would fill waiting time with reading and would even be caught reading at parties.[161] While on the campaign trail for McKinley, one of Roosevelt's daily schedules blocked out four and a half hours for reading.[162]

If Roosevelt enjoyed a book, he would attempt to befriend the author to hear more.[163]

Lesson Learned from Theodore Roosevelt

- Learn to skim and scan a book to identify essential passages.
- Always have a book with you to read when an opportunity presents itself.
- Block out times to read. Make it a priority.

President Abraham Lincoln

"I don't think much of a man who is not wiser today than he was yesterday." —ABRAHAM LINCOLN

Abraham Lincoln was the sixteenth president of the United States. Lincoln was a self-made man who rose to greatness. He did not have a lot of formal education and was self-educated. He attended school for less than a year and taught himself to read by candlelight or firelight when young.[164] He stopped going to school when he surpassed his teacher's ability.[165]

Lincoln would get up early in the morning to read the Bible.[166] He also enjoyed reading Shakespeare and poetry, sometimes at the expense of his chores.[167] For a period, his constant habit of reading at the expense of work earned him the reputation of being lazy.[168]

He always had a book with him.[169] His stepmother supported his learning and encouraged it, but his father believed it got in the way of work, yet he did not interfere with his son's learning.[170] His father "had to force his son to take up reading, but once the boy became a reader, only force could get him stopped."[171] Perhaps Lincoln discovered that reading and education were indeed ways to avoid being a farmer.

When Lincoln left home, he headed to New Salem and became its postmaster.[172] He could get an advance reading of the local newspapers in this position. He learned how to keep an eye on important issues and collect information that would later help him as he ran for office. While running a general store, Lincoln found a law book that inspired him to become a lawyer and run for public office.[173] Lincoln taught himself to be a lawyer.

Lincoln was not known to have an extensive library; instead, he borrowed books to read. Lincoln once said, "The things I want to know are in books; my best friend is the man who'll git me a book I ain't read."[174] Lincoln repeatedly read the books he owned.[175] While Lincoln read, he would capture quotes and key points in his copybook or commonplace book.[176] Lincoln was also known to read aloud because "he liked to hear the words."[177] He internalized the messages and used them throughout his political career.

Lessons Learned from Abraham Lincoln

- Make reading a priority.
- Capture essential information in a commonplace book.
- If you want to become an expert in a new field, start reading in that field.

Military Leaders

The military understands the need to prepare for the future. Servicemen and women are constantly working to improve what they know and do to meet all threats and opportunities. Each military branch has established a reading list to help its war fighters. They encourage members at all levels to take time for reading. Reading helps provide the knowledge necessary to translate it into skill.

The most successful officers have adopted a regular reading habit. For example, General Stanley McChrystal would get up early to run and listen to audiobooks.[178]

Reading helps commanders and soldiers be successful in the theater of war. Although the weapons may change, the basics of battle do not. Becoming as familiar as possible with the theater of operations will help a military leader be successful. This means reading about geography, tactics, culture, and language. As Burke notes, there are five thousand years of documented military history.[179] General George Washington required his officers to read Humphrey Bland's *A Treatise on Military Discipline* to gain the necessary knowledge to lead troops.[180] The more skill one has in one's profession, the easier it becomes to recognize patterns in activities.[181] Someone who takes the time to read, reflect, and build mental models of responses is more able to recognize the patterns and respond. This is applicable to every profession, not just the military. Someone who recognizes a change in patterns can take advantage of the change.

I regret not being a better student of the military arts. I did not read as much as I should have about my assigned profession. I have tried to make up for it since by encouraging new military officers to read as much as they can. Unfortunately, this advice is not always accepted.

An individual who can read can learn everything else.

Marine General James Mattis

"Ultimately, a real understanding of history means that we face NOTHING new under the sun."[182] —GENERAL JAMES MATTIS

Marine Gen. James Mattis, a Secretary of Defense, summed up the importance of reading as it related to his leadership:

"The problem with being too busy to read is that you learn by experience (or by your men's experience), i.e., the hard way. By reading, you learn through others' experiences, generally a better way to do business, especially in our line of work where the consequences of incompetence are so final for young men. Thanks to my reading, I have never been caught flat-footed by any situation, never at a loss for how any problem has been addressed (successfully or unsuccessfully) before. It doesn't give me all the answers, but it lights what is often a dark path ahead."[183]

General Mattis is an avid reader, and reportedly has a library of seven thousand books.[184]

Lessons Learned from General Mattis

- Read to learn about the experiences of others so you do not make their mistakes.
- Build a library that will serve you throughout your life.

General George S. Patton

General George S. Patton exemplified the importance of reading as a military officer.

Patton was a leading combat general during World War II. Yet, his career almost didn't happen because he suffered from dyslexia.[185] He struggled with school throughout his life. When he was young, an aunt helped him learn. She also nurtured his appreciation of reading, even though he found it difficult.[186] From a young age, he wanted to be in the military. Because he struggled with academics, he first went to the Virginia Military Institute. He then applied to West Point Military Academy. He took this route so he would not have to take an exam he was confident he would fail.[187] He failed his first year at West Point Military Academy. He had to overcome his disability to successfully graduate from the academy. Despite his academic challenges, he was an avid reader of military and world history.

Patton had a knack for becoming involved in important campaigns and getting influential leaders to mentor him. He positioned himself in the tank corps through these encounters. He graduated from the Command and General Staff School and the Army War College.[188] Patton would continue his studies of military history as well as advance his knowledge of the newly forming field of tank warfare.[189]

Early in his career, he purchased a library of military books that he took with him throughout his military life.[190] He referenced these books often. He would write notes in the margins as well as transcribe notes to note cards. While a cadet at West Point, he would write the names of tactics in book margins.[191]

Patton also studied the lives of past and present commanders to try to understand their thought processes.[192] He focused on the commanders he opposed in the same theater of operations. Patton would also try to understand the people with whom he was going to engage either in combat or to live among. For example, during Operation Torch (the Allied invasion of North Africa), he believed it was important to read the Koran to gain insight into the culture in North Africa.[193] Patton would convert what he read about culture, terrain, history, and military history into tactics used on the battlefield. "Patton was able to use historical knowledge and analogies to help guide his command decisions and to create a successful outcome."[194] Patton would read the works of the men he fought in battle.

An excellent example of how Patton assimilated information and used it to his advantage occurred before the Normandy invasion.[195] Patton read all six volumes of *The History of the Norman Conquest of England*, which was the history of William the Conqueror and his battles on the Brittany and Normandy peninsulas. He believed studying the road networks was a crucial aspect of the art of war. From the *Norman Conquest* books, he studied William's advances and drew the conclusion that roads had to be on passable terrain. He knew modern roads were also sited on passable terrain. When the Germans demolished the road network, he followed the same roads William the Conqueror used. After completing his study of William the Conqueror, Patton called Colonel Koch into his office and told him that the focal point of all intelligence planning was to be on Metz, France. From his personal study, Patton realized Metz was a major transportation hub they must secure. His ability to conduct a thorough terrain analysis using William the Conqueror's campaign as a model attests to his information-assimilation abilities.[196]

Patton would take everything into consideration to build mental models that would serve him in battle.[197] He would draw on his life experiences, his reading and reflection, and education. Because Patton read so much about military history, he could recognize patterns in activity as they occurred and react to them.[198] Patton wrote: "I think that it is necessary for a man to begin to read military history in its earliest and hence crudest form to follow it down in natural sequence, permitting his mind to grow with his subject until he can grasp without effort the most abstruse question of the science of war because he is already permeated with all its elements."[199]

Patton understood that one either learned lessons the hard way through personal experience or he learned from those who went before him. In a letter to his son on D-Day, Patton stressed the importance of knowing history.[200] He stressed that the dates, names, and minor details were not important, but the essence of the situation and solution were. He also encouraged his son to read biographies and autobiographies.

Not only did Patton read for self-development; he would also encourage others to read.[201] He also gave weekly lectures to the officers in his command on what he was reading.

His profound knowledge of military history also played a part while he was documenting the history of World War II.[202] As commander of the Fifteenth Army, he was responsible with "researching and writing reports on how different sections of the U.S. Army had performed during World War II."[203] Before his arrival, the unit had completed only 10 of 137 reports. Within three months, they had completed the rest.

Lessons Learned from General Patton

- Learning only about your niche is not enough; to be truly successful you must read widely.

- Learn the lessons of others, so you do not repeat their mistakes.
- Encourage reading throughout your organization.
- Create a library to help you with your decision making.

General Stanley McChrystal

General Stanley McChrystal served as the Commander of Joint Special Operations Command in Iraq. McChrystal is an avid reader who favors history and biographies.[204]

McChrystal picked up his love of reading from his mother, who enjoyed literature and the classics.[205] Reading was one of his favorite activities while a cadet at West Point Military Academy. During down time, he would read biographies and histories.

McChrystal spoke at length about his reading habits in a podcast interview.[206] Although he loved reading physical books, he switched to audiobooks to consume books under a time constraint. He combined listening to audiobooks with his daily fitness routine, so he could "read" while running and lifting weights. Because audiobooks were rare when he started to listen to them, he would listen to anything he could get his hands on. On most days, he would listen to two separate books: one while getting ready for the day in his bathroom, the other while working out. He could consume books faster during his workouts.

McChrystal indicated he did 70 percent of his reading through an audio format.[207] He purchased a subscription to Audible.com to keep a constant flow of books to his listening device. The books he chose were not all military-related; he also chose works on world issues.[208] He would listen to books related to history, trending topics, biographies, and special large-scale projects like the building of the Panama Canal. He would often binge read on a specific topic like whaling or the

Founding Fathers.[209] This provided an in-depth view on topics.

McChrystal's runs and reading breaks allowed him a brief respite from the war zone.[210] It allowed him to think about things other than his reports and mission briefs. McChrystal dedicated himself to a strict routine, where fitness and reading were central themes.[211] He believes how and what he does reflect the leadership style he wants to present.

He and his wife would visit used bookstores during his career, and he would pick up books as gifts for people with whom he served.

Lessons Learned from General McChrystal

- Adapt consumption methods to your situation.
- Supplement your workout with reading.
- Binge reading on a topic is a great way to become fluent in a new field of study.

Major Dick Winters

Major Dick Winters was one of the commanders of Easy Company of the 101st Airborne Division. His company was made famous in the HBO series *Band of Brothers*. With his men, he jumped into France during D-Day as well as into the Netherlands during Operation Market Garden. He also participated in the Battle of Bulge and the capture of Berchtesgaden. Winters's preparation for the invasion of Normandy included physical fitness, field exercises, and extensive reading. He read every tactical manual that he could find to improve his tactical knowledge. He realized the importance this knowledge would play in the days ahead. In his autobiography, *Beyond Band of Brothers*, he had this to say about the importance of reading as a military officer: "The bottom line is that leaders have entrusted to them the most precious commodity this country possesses: the lives of America's sons and daughters. Consequently, they must have a thorough understanding of their profession."[212] His preparedness helped to secure the peace in Europe during World War II.

Lesson Learned from Major Dick Winters

- Increase your competence with a regular reading habit.

Business Leaders

Most of the successful business leaders I have read about have been avid readers. Like our Founding Fathers, presidents, and military leaders, they tend to read history and biographies. They want to learn success secrets.[213] Business leaders are always reflecting on the past so they can better shape the future. They strive to learn lessons from the best in the business.[214] Business leaders who share their experiences often share information about who taught or influenced them.

According to a study of 1,200 successful business leaders, they all use reading as a self-improvement strategy.[215] "Deep, broad reading habits are often a defining characteristic of our greatest leaders and can catalyze insight, innovation, empathy, and personal effectiveness."[216]

The libraries of business leaders are like those of other leaders: They contain classic books with timeless lessons.[217] Successful leaders develop libraries filled with books to help them be more successful, whereas the general population tends to read for entertainment.[218] "Serious leaders who are serious readers build personal libraries dedicated to how to think, not how to compete."[219] Many of these libraries cost hundreds of thousands of dollars and are focused on niche topics.

While I try to read throughout the year, personalities like Bill Gates and President Obama take vacations to read and reflect. They will fill notebooks with ideas to bring back to their teams. Here are some examples of business leaders who use reading to get ahead.

Bill Gates

"I really had a lot of dreams when I was a kid, and I think a great deal of that grew out of the fact that I had a chance to read a lot."

—BILL GATES

Bill Gates, cofounder of Microsoft and philanthropist, is an avid reader. He reads at least an hour each night and a couple of hours each weekend. He likes to read newspapers, magazines, books, and reports to stay current on world and technology affairs. He tries to read a newspaper daily and at least one weekly news magazine each week. When he was young, he read so much his parents established a rule that he could not read while dinner was on the table.

Gates enjoys reading biographies and autobiographies.[220] He likes to read about business leaders and scientists, seeing the paths people took to achieve the levels of success they did. Additionally, he likes to read science fiction, history, and even the encyclopedia. He reads fifty or more books each year.[221]

Every year, Gates takes a vacation called "Think Week" to catch up on reading and generate ideas for moving his business forward.[222] During this personal retreat, Gates spends up to fifteen hours each day for two weeks reading. He reads from a variety of sources, looking for ideas that will improve his business. He does not socialize with anyone during this time. The result of this personal retreat is a set of messages, notes, and emails to help guide his staff.

He shares what he has read and his thoughts through a website called Gatesnotes.[223]

Lessons Learned from Bill Gates

- Take mini-holidays simply to read and reflect.
- Share what you are reading with everyone around you.
- Dedicate part of your day to reading.

Thomas Edison

Thomas Edison was an inventor extraordinaire, who helped create the modern world. He held 1,093 patents during his lifetime.[224]

His youth shaped him for a life of reading and exploration. Edison was the last of seven children; all the others were at least fifteen years older. Thus, he received a lot of personal attention from his parents.[225] Early in life, he suffered from scarlet fever and became partly deaf. He did not begin to speak until he was four years old.[226] According to some accounts, he was also dyslexic.[227] These limitations held him back, and he did not start school until he was ten. Despite his limitations, he was very curious about the world and how it worked.[228] Unfortunately, Edison was too inquisitive for school and became a nuisance to the sole teacher. His mother pulled him out of school and homeschooled him.[229] She helped him overcome his dyslexia and gain a solid foundation in reading, writing, and math.[230] Edison became a fan of world history, English literature, and poetry.

"His interest in science was first sparked when his mother bought him his first scientific book, *The School of Natural Philosophy*. He studied the book and performed all the experiments described in it at home. He soon set up his own laboratory in his room and began performing original experiments."[231]

His mother introduced him to the library when he was eleven years old.[232] Although he seemed intent on reading every book in the stacks, his parents shaped his reading interests. His father encouraged him to read the classics and sciences. Once his mother taught him everything she could, he moved on to self-directed learning.

Edison worked as a newsboy on the Grand Trunk Railroad. During layovers in Detroit, he would visit the library to read science books and journals.[233] With library card number thirty-three, he was one of the first to use the Detroit Free Library.[234] He continued to read at the library as he advanced in his career. During this period, he experimented with telegraph technology: transmitters and receivers, electrical systems, and chemical batteries.

"As a home-schooled, self-educated youth, Edison learned lessons that were to serve him all his life. He learned education was his own responsibility, he learned to take initiative, he learned to be persistent, and he learned he could gain practical knowledge, inspiration and wisdom by reading books."[235]

Edison had a high level of focus and perseverance, which would help him succeed as an inventor.[236] Edison's love of reading and independent learning style helped him overcome his lack of a secondary education and physical limitations. According to Edison, his deafness drove him to read to gain knowledge.[237] Through reading and experimentation, he excelled in electrical science, mechanics, chemical analysis, and manufacturing.[238]

"When I want to discover something, I begin by reading up everything that has been done along that line in the past—that's what all these books in the library are for. I see what has been accomplished at great labor and expense in the past. I gather data of many thousands of experiments as a starting point, and then I make thousands more."[239]

Lessons Learned from Thomas Edison

- If you want to gain deep knowledge about a topic, read about it.
- Public and academic libraries are great places to learn.

Mark Zuckerberg

Mark Zuckerberg, the founder and CEO of Facebook, completed a personal quest called "A Year of Books."[240] Zuckerberg vowed to read two books per month and post them to his book club. The books focused on different cultures, history, beliefs, and technologies.[241] During this Year of Books, he discussed selected books on a Facebook page.[242] He would share recommended books and provide his comments. Followers of the Facebook page could add their comments. He even invited authors to discuss the books through posts, live question-and-answer sessions, and Facebook Live video events. As described on the Facebook page "A Year of Books": "We will read a new book every two weeks and discuss it here. Our books will emphasize learning about new cultures, beliefs, histories and technologies."

Zuckerberg recognizes that reading even for fun can result in more productivity. This is in part due to a reduced stress level and increased level of concentration.[243]

Lessons Learned from Mark Zuckerberg

- Establish reading goals.
- Share your reading goals with others and invite them to participate.

Elon Musk

Elon Musk is another very successful business leader who has revolutionized many industries, including electric cars, solar power, and space travel. He also has a heavy appetite for reading and is self-taught on most topics. Like Lincoln and Edison, he outpaced his teacher's knowledge.[244]

According to his brother, Musk reads two books a day.[245] Musk developed his appetite for books when he was young. By the time he was eight, he ran out of things to read at the library.[246] By the time he was twelve, he completed a workbook on programming in three days; the workbook should have taken six months to complete. With that knowledge, he wrote and sold a game called *Blastar*.[247] Bullied in school, he turned to books for solace.[248] When Musk was in his teens, he read about ten hours per day on a myriad of topics. He enjoyed reading philosophy, religion, nonfiction, fiction, and biographies.[249] He would also immerse himself in encyclopedias.

Musk learned to build rockets by reading books.[250] He borrowed all of Jim Cantrell's books on rocket propulsion.[251] He also taught himself aerospace, programming, and automotive engineering.

Lessons Learned from Elon Musk

- Read widely. You never know what ideas will combine with others.
- Quickly gain knowledge on a topic by reading as much as you can on it.

Mark Cuban

Mark Cuban is a successful businessman, author, inventor, and philanthropist. He attributes part of his success to the fact that he is willing to read more than others.[252] This habit started when he was young. He would stay up until the middle of the night reading about collecting baseball cards and stamps.[253] The knowledge he gained helped him make money trading cards.

Cuban reads at least three hours each day.[254] He would read every book, magazine, or report he could that was relevant to his business.[255] He sees reading as a strategy to gain a competitive advantage.[256] Cuban points out that everything he reads is available to all. The difference between him and his competition is that he reads more.[257] He shares that the best investments he makes is purchasing and reading books.[258] At a cost of less than $20, he can find an idea that leads to new customers or business. This more than pays for the book.

Lessons Learned from Mark Cuban

- The knowledge you seek can be found in a bookstore or library.
- Read daily to stay abreast of new trends and research.
- Out-read your competition.

Warren Buffett

Warren Buffett, chairman and chief executive officer of Berkshire Hathaway, spends 80 percent of his day reading.[259] He claims to read five to six hundred pages per day. During the workday, he reads business reports and financial papers such as the *Wall Street Journal* and *Financial Times*. He reads books and newspapers in the evening. He can do this because he has mastered speed-reading. Buffett reads to find new opportunities and strategies for investing.[260]

When asked how to get smarter about business, Buffett said, "Read five hundred pages like this every day. That's how knowledge works. It builds up, like compound interest. All of you can do it, but I guarantee not many of you will."[261]

Lessons Learned from Warren Buffett

- Read every day.
- Read to find opportunities for growth.

Oprah Winfrey

Oprah Winfrey is a leader in the media industry. She has loved reading for as long as she can remember. Even though she grew up in poverty, her stepmother and father understood the value of education. They required her to read library books and do weekly book reports.[262] She credits reading as a child to her success as an adult. She said, "Had I not had books and education in Mississippi, I would have believed that's all there was."[263]

She read five books per week while preparing for her television talk show in 1987.[264]

Her love of reading inspired her to start a reading club as part of her television show.[265] Oprah has inspired others to read through her continuous encouragement and exposure to authors and books.[266] Her influence can immediately put a book on the bestseller list. Oprah also sends free books to libraries that partner with her book club.[267] She has also gone on to build a $40 million Leadership Academy for Girls with a modern library.

Lesson Learned from Oprah Winfrey

- Share your love of reading with others.

Dolly Parton

The famous country singer Dolly Parton, also known as the "book lady," has a special place in her heart for literacy. According to the singer, she grew up dirt poor in rural Tennessee.[268] Her father grew up illiterate and ashamed. This bothered Parton throughout her life. She claims her father was very intelligent, but illiteracy held him back. To honor her father, she started the Imagination Library in 1995. This program provides a free book each month to children up to five years of age.[269]

According to Pellot, the Imagination Library program has helped children in 1,400 communities in the United States, Canada, and Australia.[270] The program donates approximately 1 million books per month and has donated over 100 million books so far.[271]

Lesson Learned from Dolly Parton

- Build company libraries and virtual libraries to support those around you.

Wrap Up

As Michael Hyatt notes in his article "5 Ways Reading Makes You a Better Leader," many who are successful leaders are also avid readers. Successful leaders realize reading provides them with ideas and direction. It also helps keep them from making unnecessary mistakes.

The leaders presented in this chapter achieved greatness in large part due to their love of reading. Many created their own reference libraries as they formed governments, built rockets, or won battles. These successful leaders read to learn about topics of interest, to stay current, to avoid the mistakes of others, to share their learning with others, and even to relax. Developing a regular reading habit was essential to their success and should be a foundation for anyone's success.

There are many benefits to reading in addition to gaining knowledge. The next chapter explores these benefits.

CHAPTER FOUR

Benefits of Reading

As we saw in chapter three, many influential leaders believed in the power of reading. They recognized the benefits of developing a regular reading habit. However, a high percentage of adults will not read another book in their entire lives, so why should you consider doing so?

Reading is not just about acquiring knowledge or entertainment; there are many benefits from reading. Reading can improve mental and physical health, as well as a person's ability to meet and overcome obstacles and appreciate other cultures. Reading can help you achieve personal and professional success, which can lead to advances in your career.

There may not be another single activity that can affect one's life so much. Developing a regular reading habit will change an individual.[272] What one does and how one thinks about things will change as new information is gained. Because of reading, I am not the same person I was ten years ago, or even one year ago. Reading is an activity that can help you improve, but you must be an active participant.[273] I look at reading as a patch to my personal operating system. "Broad and deep reading habits can sharpen intelligence, make you a better communicator, and improve emotional intelligence, among other benefits—proving that readers are indeed, leaders."[274] Let's explore the many ways reading is beneficial to professionals.

"The art of reading is in great part that of acquiring a better understanding of life from one's encounter with it in a book." —ANDRÉ MAUROIS

As Ben Franklin once said, "Early to bed and early to rise, makes a man healthy, wealthy, and wise." The same applies to reading. A steady reading diet will boost one's health, wealth, and wisdom. Let's first look at the health benefits.

Reading Improves Health

People rarely consider the health benefits associated with reading. Research shows reading as a regular activity can add years to one's life.

Reading for more than three and a half hours per week, or around half an hour a day, results in a 20 percent extension of life expectancy compared to those who do not read, according to research published in the *Social Science and Medicine* journal.[275] The study determined this was a two-year lifespan increase compared to nonreaders. However, you can't just read anything for those three and a half hours; reading books is the key. Researchers emphasized that reading books provided increased longevity over those who read magazines or newspapers.[276]

Reading Is an Active Exercise That Uses the Brain
Watching TV is a passive exercise that does not stimulate much brain activity. Reading, on the other hand, is an intense mental activity—a gymnasium for the mind.[277] Reading requires engagement with memory as one assigns meaning to what is read. The brain craves the type of exercise reading provides.[278] Reading enhances analytical skills such as recognizing patterns.[279] Active reading will strengthen the neu-

ral connections in the brain tied to vision, learning, and language.[280] Reading can also slow the effects of Alzheimer's, dementia, stress, and depression;[281] keeping the brain active can help stave off these illnesses.[282]

The way one reads also has an impact on acumen. Reading a printed book reinforces skills different than those used while using an e-reader.[283] Readers tend to read the first line and then skim down the left-hand margin while using an e-reader. Reading comprehension on an e-reader is not as strong as when reading a printed book.[284] Focusing on a novel is more difficult for someone who does a lot of e-reading. Reading a printed book thirty to forty-five minutes a day strengthens linear reading skills.

Reading Can Help Improve Physical Health

Reading not only strengthens one's brain and increases longevity; if done right, it can improve your physical health as well. Workouts are more likely to last longer if you're reading a book while on an elliptical trainer, stationary bike, or treadmill.[285] This increased physical activity leads to improved health. I find it difficult to read while moving, but I do stay focused on podcasts or audiobooks. As we learned in the last chapter, switching to audiobooks enabled General Stanley McChrystal to strengthen his body and squeeze more into his day.

Disconnecting from electronic devices and reading a printed book an hour before going to bed improves sleep. Of course, that depends upon what is read. Some books would definitely keep me up late. Although reading a digital book can help you relax, reading with an e-reader on an iPad or smartphone can actually prevent one from getting adequate sleep.[286] The blue light of an e-reader hampers the body's production of melatonin, which is needed for restful sleep.[287]

Installing and using applications that adjust the blue light for nighttime reading can offset this negative effect. On the other hand, dedicated e-readers such as the Amazon Kindle use e-ink and do not use the blue light.[288]

Studies also show reading helps people feel better about life and themselves.[289] One added benefit is that reading helps you appear more intelligent, and thus more attractive.[290]

Reading Improves Wealth

When thinking about reading to improve wealth, consider the information from books that will help you become more successful. Books are a quick way to gather the lessons learned from others as well as helping to avoid making the mistakes others have made, which in turn saves money. Books can provide enough background knowledge for different aspects of a career. Books help generate new ideas by providing a vast array of solutions from which to choose and combine. Books help us function in society, providing ample topics for discussion.

Reading Can Help You Be More Successful

Reading allows you to stand on the shoulders of those who have walked before you. There are three ways to benefit from reading about others: discovering new ideas and methods, learning about struggles others have had, and learning how they succeeded.[291] Successful leaders take time to analyze how other leaders worked. They take time to learn from the mistakes of those who went before them. In the article "What You Didn't Know About the Act of Reading Books," Shane Parrish highlights the writings of Machiavelli and Seneca, who noted there is much to learn from those who have traveled before us.[292]

Taking time to think about what is being read and not merely assuming the thoughts of the author is important. We need to digest, synthesize, and organize the thoughts of others in order to understand. This is the grunt work of thinking. It's how we acquire wisdom.

Reading about the paths of those who have gone before us not only helps us navigate a quicker path; the stories also can motivate and inspire us. We must put into action what we learn. I am weaving new ideas into my personal endeavors daily. Reading can also help advance ideas in the workplace. If you're trying to put in place something new or you need support for a decision, you can cite articles and books supporting a decision.

Reading Can Help Advance a Career

For most jobs, reading is a prerequisite for advancement in a career field.[293] Reading helps one gather reports and conduct research.

The better you can read, the more worlds you can enter. Being able to read the jargon and understand the lexicon of a specific profession can open doors for that profession. Readers can better use the advice professional experts provide.

> "You are the average of the five people you spend the most time with."
> —JIM ROHN

By spending time with successful entrepreneurs, business leaders, and influential people, a reader will in turn raise his or her game.[294] Reading is one of the cheapest ways to improve operations. I frequently pick up books to fill my knowledge gaps.

Reading Can Help Save Money

Reading can help you save money by allowing you to learn from the experiences of others. Business books share insights on how to not make business mistakes. Management books help prevent costly personnel mistakes. How-to books share tips for accomplishing tasks with less time and money. Why go down the road of hard knocks when others have laid out a path for you?

Ideas that can solve a myriad of problems are available in $20 books. It is one of the cheapest idea generators out there. Buying used books can also save extra money. I have purchased many books for pennies by searching Amazon's used-books marketplace.

Become More Creative

Reading provides an opportunity to set one's life on pause. Readers have an opportunity to stop thinking about problems and challenges and look at what others have overcome. As exposure increases new ways to think about things, readers in turn start developing innovative solutions to their own problems. They can pull ideas from many disciplines and combine them into new solutions.

Nonfiction is not the only place to gather ideas. By reading about fictional worlds, the writer can only provide so much detail; one's mind fills in the voids with imagination. A reader must use creative thinking to appreciate what fiction has to offer.

The act of reading is a fascinating mental process. Readers are translating abstract shapes (letters) into words, sentences, and paragraphs, and then assigning meaning to them.[295] It's a complex, powerful skill that leads to comprehension, inference, and creative stimulation. Reading strengthens mental processes.

Reading Can Help You Function in Society

At a very basic level, reading helps people function in society.[296] Reading allows us to understand everything from food labels to policies. Being able to read lets a reader adapt to his or her environment. Traveling to a foreign country without knowing the language can be quite unsettling. Reading helps us develop a comfort level in new situations. A reader will be banking ideas, stories, and concepts for use in conversation with others.[297] The more variety a reader takes in, the greater his or her conversation palette will be.[298] The more varied your reading list is, the better chance you will have something to contribute to a conversation.

Individuals who cannot read are dependent upon those who can.[299] As a result, others can subject them to manipulation. Some governments try to suppress education and reading for this reason. Research has shown that individuals who read self-help books realize they need to take responsibility for their own lives.[300] They also learn they are not the only ones who have the same concerns.

Reading Is Good for Self-Esteem

Reading increases a person's level of expertise. This increased level of expertise results in a higher level of self-esteem.[301] A reader feels more confident. Individuals who are illiterate or are poor readers often feel bad about themselves.[302] Because they are unable to read, they also tend to underperform in many subjects. Illiteracy holds people back from better jobs. Illiteracy also affects quality-of-life issues such as personal health.

Reading Can Be a Beneficial Challenge

A reader will need to develop a plan and set goals to be successful. Setting a reading goal can help not only on a personal level, but also on a professional level. "Challenges help to build internal motivation, confidence, discipline, and willpower."[303]

Reading Improves Wisdom

Perhaps the most important benefit of reading is that it is a means for acquiring new knowledge and, over time, wisdom. Readers can receive lessons shared by others through the simple process of reading the words on a page; however, they not only learn what is shared; they also develop culturally, increase vocabulary, and build mental skills.

Reading Helps Us Learn

Someone who can read has the skills to learn everything else. Do not consider learning as an activity that happens only in college or under the watchful eye of an instructor. Readers are in control of their learning. They are in charge of setting their own curriculums.[304]

Reading is a cost-effective way to learn how to do many things. Adults buy millions of self-help books each year, and many of them find value from what they are reading.[305] Perhaps the reason you picked up this book was to help you improve your reading to become more successful. After all, successful leaders use reading to improve and learn across their lifetime. Learning is cumulative. No one can take knowledge from you; thus, you are always able to improve your status in life.

Reading is a cheap, efficient, and effective way to prepare for a new task. When I want to learn something new, I will first read extensively on a topic to get a feel for it, before I try to tackle it myself. This has been my modus operandi for learning everything, including magic, martial arts, web mastering, programming, instructional design, and even serving on a board of trustees.

Through reading, individuals can become an expert in their fields. "If you read an hour a day, one book per week, you will be an expert in your field within three years."[306] Besides building their own formal education curriculum at a fraction of the cost, readers allow themselves to learn at their own pace. In one study, the following was determined:

> It is demonstrated that virtually all of these readers believe they learned something important from the self-help book they read, that three-quarters of them claim to have changed some aspect of their day-to-day life as a result of their reading, and that over half of them are able to describe concrete actions which they undertook in response to suggestions provided by the authors of self-help books.[307]

I had put together a degree program on web mastering without formal education on the topic. As I learned how to be a webmaster, I read many books on the topic and worked through countless problems. I believe I got a better education on this topic than I would have in a classroom setting because it was very personal to me. Besides maintaining my position at the college, I used self-directed learning to acquire new skills, and created my new business, which uses social media to help other small businesses. As I wrote this book, I read many books on self-publishing, learned how to use Scrivener, and learned about writing for publication. If you wish to broaden your knowledge on a topic, do a deep dive on that topic and read as much as possible.

Expand Culturally

Reading not only helps you obtain knowledge and skill on a specific topic; it can also help you learn about other cultures and people. Reading allows a glimpse into a different culture or part of the world. With reading, you can travel to the future and the past.

"Books allow you to experience other people, other places, and other cultures that you might never be exposed to in regular life. This helps you develop compassion for suffering, empathy for those different than you, and an open mind."[308]

Have you ever felt you were familiar with a place because of the descriptions you had read in a book? I have. When I was young, I used to read a lot of westerns, specifically those of Louis L'Amour. When I first moved west to Cheyenne, Wyoming, and traveled throughout the missile field, I had an opportunity to see and experience the vistas L'Amour described. I felt I had already seen them. I had this feeling also in part because my wife and I listened to Ken Burns's *The West*. We traveled across the states on the same paths as original settlers.

According to President Obama and Michael Hyatt, leaders can improve their people skills by reading.[309] Reading helps improve emotional intelligence. Leaders should not only read nonfiction books on leadership, history, and business; they should also read captivating novels.[310] Stories are powerful vehicles to convey effective methods for relating with fellow human beings. "Reading helps promote respect for and tolerance of others' views."[311] People who read are also more engaged in their communities culturally and as voters.[312] Referring to a National Education Association survey, Cornell University provost Carolyn Martin wrote: "People who read for pleasure are many times more likely than those who do not to visit museums and attend concerts, and almost three times as likely to perform volunteer and charity work. Readers are active participants in the world around them, and that engagement is critical to individual and social well-being."[313]

Books Build Mental Skills

Reading is like going to the gym for the brain. Reading helps develop many important skills, such as focus, discipline, memory, critical analysis, and vocabulary. Reading not only helps raise intelligence; it also boosts verbal and emotional skills.

Focus and Discipline

Daily, we are distracted with ads, pop-ups, and commercials while reading content on the web, in magazines, and on TV. Reading books provides an opportunity to focus. A regular reading routine can increase power of concentration.[314] This increased focus can lead to relaxation and decreased level of stress; reading can be more beneficial to relieving stress than listening to music or playing video games.[315]

By setting aside time to read a book and focusing on the task of reading, you're building self-discipline. This is a skill you can apply in many other settings.

Strengthen Memory

While reading a book, you are forced to remember key elements. Each memory causes activity in the brain. As you read, you're strengthening your brain's neural networks.[316] And the more you exercise your memory, the better it will become.

Develop Critical Thinking

A reader must also exercise analytical and critical thinking skills, problem-solving skills, and a sense of judgment. You must analyze the plot if reading fiction or map out the structure of the argument if reading nonfiction. Business leaders take reading seriously as a way to help them think better.

Increase Vocabulary

Reading and vocabulary go hand in hand. Reading is perhaps the best way to develop a stronger vocabulary.[317] Reading exposes a person to more unique words than television.[318] Wise notes that children will pick up 50 percent more words from reading than from watching television.[319] From an early age, we learn how to determine the meaning of a word based on its context.[320]

A better vocabulary will help you write and speak more effectively. An increased vocabulary will also help you organize more complex thoughts.

A strong vocabulary can be beneficial in almost any profession. The more versed a person is in the jargon of a profession, the better he or she will able to communicate. This can lead to better-paying jobs and career advancement. You should seek to continue to improve your vocabulary through reading.

Improve Your Writing

"If you want to be a writer, you must do two things above all others: read a lot and write a lot." —STEPHEN KING

Reading helps develop many important skills that will help with writing: developing a larger vocabulary and seeing how others deliver their content.[321] As musicians are inspired by listening to the music of others, reading the works of a specific author or genre can influence an individual's style of writing.[322]

Writing is also a key means of communication. The better a person can write, the better he or she can communicate ideas. Reading is the receiving of an idea and writing is the sharing of an idea. You cannot be part of the communication process if you struggle with reading.[323] You must learn to read and write if you want to learn the lessons of the world and contribute to the world's knowledge.

Free or Cheap Entertainment

Reading can be a very cheap, or even free, form of entertainment or education, especially if using one's local library or a used bookstore. Reading a book offers the best bang for the buck compared to going to the movies, going out to eat, or other forms of entertainment.[324] Selecting a variety of books can take you on adventures to faraway places and to unimaginable fantasy worlds, with the price of the ticket being the cost of a book. People can save a tremendous amount of money on the cost of a formal education by developing their own curriculum and using the local library as the source of books.

You can choose what to do with your time. You can surf the internet and play mindless games, or you can level up your life with a nonfiction book or immerse yourself in a good work of fiction.

Wrap Up

There are many benefits to reading. Reading not only helps increase knowledge on a subject; it can improve your health and fatten your pocketbook. A regular reading habit can pay dividends greater than what is paid for a book. Little wonder so many successful people make reading a priority.

In the next chapter, we'll look at strategies for developing a reading habit. This will include setting goals, having books on hand to read, and finding time to read.

CHAPTER FIVE

Developing a Reading Habit

There are many benefits to reading, in addition to gaining knowledge. However, you will not be able to take advantage of these benefits if you are not actively reading. This chapter will share ideas for developing a reading habit. In this chapter, you will find ideas for:

- setting a reading goal,
- building a reading list,
- finding time to achieve reading goals, and
- maximizing reading.

Set a Reading Goal

As with anything else in life, if it's not measured, a person will not do it. Establish a reading goal for the year. A goal will help develop a regular reading habit. In setting a goal, you must first define your needs. For example, if you need to develop a new skill or gain specific knowledge on a topic, read on that topic.

Break Down the Goal

Begin by challenging yourself with reading a certain number of books per year. For example, I have set my sights on at least sixty books for this year. Setting a high goal is more likely to stimulate you to accept the challenge; low goals usually result in low achievements.

However, an overwhelming goal can seem daunting. Break your goal down into manageable chunks. Let's say you're setting a lofty reading goal of fifty books for the year. If you read thirty pages a day, you could finish a two-hundred-page book in a week. "The number of books you wish to read per year is equal to half the number of minutes you read per day."[325]

The goal is not set in stone and can be adjusted. When I first set my goal, I believed I could read two books per month. When the half-year mark arrived, I realized I was on track for a larger number, so I increased my goal. In 2016, I pulled together a collection of twenty-four physical books to read. As I reached the halfway point, I had read twenty-three books, but the books were not all from my original stack. Some were e-books on my iPad, and others I had purchased along the way. From my original stack, I had reached the halfway point.

Starting a Reading Habit

If you've gotten out of the habit of reading, starting with thirty pages a day could be overwhelming and may cause you to quit. Instead, start even smaller, with a goal of just one page per night (though you may read more). If you commit to at least one page per night, you can easily achieve success, which will lead to larger goals when the habit is stronger.

Here are other tips for developing a reading goal:

- Do not try to develop too many habits at once.

- Work on one or two habits at a time.
- Stack habits: link one habit to another, such as opening the book next to the bed.
- Set aside ten minutes a day to read, and then increase the time each day until you reach an hour a day.[326]
- Set aside time to read at least ten pages per day.[327]

Track What You Read

You must take on the responsibility for what and how much you are reading to maximize the effectiveness of your reading habit. A person can track the number of pages read each day, the amount of time spent reading, or log when a book is finished. I keep track with two strategies. I write a book review on my blog for all books I have completed. I also track with Goodreads the books I have read, am reading, and want to read. I am never lacking something to read. Note: Goodreads is a web-based program dedicated to tracking what one reads as well as sharing with others.

While I advocate making a goal and tracking progress, you should always pursue quality and personal growth over quantity. Endeavor to absorb the essence of what you are reading.

Read with Others

Readers can increase accountability by making their goals public, at least to their friends. The abovementioned Goodreads is an excellent program you can use to share reading progress. Developing a community around reading pursuits is a great way to help achieve goals. Reading mates can help hold you accountable for reading goals.

Getting Books to Read

You should not have to look around for something to read. Part of a reading habit is building a reading list.

Put Together a Reading List

There are many ways to create a reading list. You can add books you want to read to a paper list or in a notebook. I prefer to track what I want to read with digital lists. My favorite tool is Goodreads. Goodreads allows me to track what I want to read, what I am reading, and what I have read. However, it's not the only method. You can also make a note in Evernote, use a bullet journal, or save a listing to Diigo. I provide more information about these programs in the chapter on sharing.

It's important to create a system that is as simple as possible. Learn to immediately add books to your list when you learn of a new book or find one you want to read. That way, you'll always have a list of books to read.

Some programs, such as Evernote and Diigo, allow you to update the list with an email. Another option is to create a Gmail account for your book list, and send an email to that address every time you come across a book you want to read. Because I have Goodreads available to me on all my devices, I add new books to this list.

If you have developed a community of readers, ask for recommendations from others. Receiving personal reviews from a reading group may help in adding to a list of books.

Buy Books in Advance

Make developing a new habit as easy as possible. Have an inventory of books on hand so when one is finished, you can immediately open the next. This is something I do. When I go to a conference, I stock up on a couple of hundred dollars' worth of new books. This then becomes part of my goal for the upcoming months.

Always Have a Book on Hand

You never know when you might have a block of free time, so make sure you always have book with you. These free blocks of time may be while waiting for a flight, waiting for a medical appointment, or during lunch. Fill these empty blocks with reading. I bring a book with me if I know I will be waiting on someone or doing something like getting the oil changed in my car.

Make the development of the reading habit as easy as possible by ensuring quick availability. Have a book ready to read where you plan to read it. For example, place a book on a nightstand for bedtime reading. Because I read at lunch, I set a book next to my keys and grab both on my way to work. Place books in various locations around the house or workplace. Place a book in the car, your briefcase, or your jacket pocket. Some of those locations may also include the electronic devices you carry every day. Load your cell phone or iPad with audiobooks or e-books. I always have something to read on my phone and iPad. On each of these devices, I have the Kindle app loaded.

I will often be reading two books at the same time. Others also suggest reading more than one book at a time.[328] Some individuals read eight to ten books at a time, depending upon the mood they are in. Sometimes you want to escape with a good novel rather than focus on a serious nonfiction book.

Automating a Reading List

Using a program called If This Then That (IFTTT) may help save time and effort creating lists or even content to read when using other programs such as Evernote. IFTTT is a web-based service that connects two programs together. This allows automation of processes one would otherwise spend time doing by hand. For example, you could collect *New York Times* bestseller lists into Evernote without having to copy and paste them.

IFTTT uses a recipe that has three ingredients: a channel that outputs information, a trigger, and a channel action that inputs information. Here is an example using the *New York Times* and Evernote. Something happens with the first channel, such as the *New York Times* publishes a new bestseller list. The new list would be the trigger and cause the next action. In this case, Evernote (the second channel) records the new list. While going into the details of IFTTT is beyond the scope of this book, I can assure you that it is quite easy to set up.

Finding Time to Read

In an early survey of executives, 10 percent indicated they did not read and only 21 percent read one to six books a year.[329] They cited lack of time as the main reason for not reading or reading less. Many people use this excuse today. They have not decided reading is a priority. If you want to read more, set it as a priority. Once you do that, you can then allocate time to this priority.

Set Aside a Specific Time to Read

Time to read will not appear on its own. If you establish reading as a priority, you must set aside time to read. Time-management experts recommend creating a block of time on a calendar to read. This helps to establish it as a priority. Once it's blocked off, however, you must use it as intended. President Theodore Roosevelt would schedule thirty- to sixty-minute reading periods throughout his day.[330] At the end of his day, he would have read approximately four and a half hours. One CEO scheduled reading time using a Google calendar to read one hundred books in a year.[331] He also recommends using the Google calendar goals feature to help stay on track.

Another strategy is to tie the new habit of reading to a habit you already have in place.[332] For example, you can set aside time to read before or after a meal. J. N. Widdon, CEO and author of *The Old School Advantage: Timeless Tools for Every Generation*, recommends starting each day reading.[333] By reading first thing in the morning, you're dedicating time for self-improvement before you dedicate time to others.

Many reading periods can be set aside throughout the day based on purpose and mood. Not all time periods are equal. For example, if you have to focus intensely on what you're reading, select a time when you're most alert, such as in the morning. You might dedicate one reading time to professional reading, such as business or professional journals, while another time can be dedicated to reading books related to nonfiction professional development. You might also dedicate time to read for enjoyment and relaxation.

If you want to get the whole family involved in reading, try dedicating one hour of the day to reading engaging the whole family.

Opportunities to Read throughout the Day

There are usually many free ten- to fifteen-minute slots throughout the day. You can squeeze in an article, a blog post or two, or a few pages of a book during these time periods. Throughout the day, I will also read short articles from blogs, magazines, or those found through my personal learning network.

Look for opportunities to read throughout the day. It may be while sitting waiting for a dentist or some other appointment. Dedicate evenings to reading rather than watching television. If you're not willing to forego television, read during commercials. Read while sitting in the back seat of an Uber during rush hour. Take a book into the bathroom stall, even at work. Five to ten minutes here and there adds up. Consider stocking up on articles for those periods when you don't have time to read a whole book.

Exercising is another time to use for reading or listening to an audiobook. Reading physical books is more appropriate for treadmills, stationary bikes, and elliptical machines. Listening to an audiobook is more flexible—you can even swim with some audiobook players! I like to listen to podcasts while walking.

A lunch period is another great time to spend relaxing and reading. A habit I have recently picked up is reading during my lunch hour. I either have a physical book or Kindle book handy. I can read one to two books a week this way.

Read During the Evening

I dedicate evenings to reading rather than watching television. An average person watches three to four hours of television each evening.[334] That is twenty-one to twenty-eight hours per week that could be used to advance his or her knowledge base with a good book. Approximately one book a week could be completed if you dedicate one or two hours to reading each night.

Another great time to read is before bedtime. Reading is a great way to unwind from the day and relax.

Read When You Can

In addition to finding time to read during the day and evening, as already mentioned, note that a great deal can be read during free moments, such as waiting for someone to arrive, between appointments, walking the dog, doing dishes, and waiting in line. Author Jeff Goins recommends reading "in the margins."[335] Five or ten minutes here and there builds up to quite a bit of accomplished reading. You can read three or four books per week by taking advantage of extra free time in the day. Goins also has a business to run and a life to live. To maximize his reading, he will get a printed and audio copy from the library, as well as a Kindle version, all at the same time to maximize his opportunity to read his selection.

Commutes

Commutes can be a great time to catch up on some "reading," even when driving. You can consume many books on a daily commute with an audiobook subscription. According to research, listening to an audiobook offers many of the same benefits as reading a physical copy.[336]

Setting Aside a Reading Day or Retreat

If you're unable to set aside time each day for reading, consider setting aside a reading day once or twice a week. Another way to recharge your knowledge batteries is to take a personal reading retreat. Many leaders take time to focus on reading. As noted earlier, Bill Gates takes a two-week personal retreat dedicated to reading and gathering new ideas.

E-Reading Devices

There are many ways to maximize time for reading. For example, with an iPad, Kindle, Nook, or tablet, books are at the ready wherever you are. Most e-reading devices offer the ability to convert text to speech. A person may use a text-to-speech program that reads the book aloud.[337] This can be a great way to consume a book while driving, exercising, or involved with another activity. A program like Text2Go converts text to speech and creates a file that you can then listen to on an MP3 player, iPod, iPhone, or iPad.[338]

Eliminate Time Sinks

In a blog post called *The Best Way to Find More Time to Read*, Shane Parrish explains how he can make time to read three to five books per week.[339] He has eliminated time sinks such as watching television, unnecessary travel to work, and unscheduled shopping events. He estimates he has reclaimed twenty-five hours each week that he would have otherwise wasted. "That's 1,500 minutes. That's huge. If you read a page a minute, that's 1,500 pages a week."[340] Remember that these choices are connected to developing goals, setting priorities, and creating new habits.

Some recommend removing specific activities to make more time for reading. Dropping television is one of the most recommended.[341]

Gaming applications installed on phones and tablets are another set of considerations to consider dropping. This is not to say you shouldn't watch television or play games; rather, do these activities in moderation.

Instead of jumping on the internet to look at Facebook or Twitter streams, read fifty pages of a good book.[342] If you spend a lot of time in front of a computer, the break from the screen could provide the recharge you need to dive back into work.

One way to find more time in a schedule is to keep track of current time usage.[343] Short blocks of time for squeezing in more time for reading could be identified if you keep accurate records. Successful leaders always manage to find time for reading. Many have a book with them all the time to sneak in a little extra reading during the day.

Tips for Achieving a Goal

Even if there is a stack of books sitting next to you and you have time to read, you may still struggle to complete your book goal. Here are some more tips to help.

Do Not Force Yourself to Read a Bad Book

If you find yourself reading a terrible book—stop! Do not waste time continuing to read because you feel you have an obligation to finish the book. If you don't have the urge to take notes while reading nonfiction, stop. If a novel is boring, find another. After all, you'd change the television channel or radio station if the show was not serving your needs. A book is no different. Sometimes reading a chapter or two is sufficient if you're trying to solve a problem. There is no need to read the entire book.

Time is money, goes the adage, and you cannot afford to waste time and money reading bad books. You must learn to discern what a good book is and what is not worth reading.

Take time to review the book before investing in it. Will the book share practical experience to help you solve your problem? Will the book help you develop skills to gain a competitive advantage? Learning to choose books worth your time will also help you learn who gives worthwhile book recommendations.

Since many successful people read nonfiction and fiction, reading books that make you feel good is important. Find something that you enjoy, and there is a greater chance you will finish it.

Create a Quiet Place to Read

When reading for an extended time, it is imperative to have a conducive environment. Reading when there are a lot of distractions is difficult. If possible, find a quiet place to dedicate to reading. This place should have a comfortable reading chair with adequate light. Keep the book out after reading a chapter or two rather than putting it out of sight.

Add Variety to a Reading List

Add variety to a reading list, not only in genre, but also length. As *Lifehack* author Justin Miller noted, "constantly reading longer books was taking its toll, so I wanted to make sure I stayed consistent; by choosing a few shorter reads."[344]

Selecting a format you enjoy will contribute to success. This format could be an e-book, print book, or audiobook. And remember that you don't have to stick to books. Read content based on the mood and time available; this may mean you only have the time to read blogs, newspapers, or journal articles. Remember, Warren Buffett read five hundred pages a day, which included newspapers and reports, as well as books.

Find a Reading Buddy

Besides developing a group or community of readers to share goals and titles, it is helpful to connect with a reading buddy. Everything is more fun when there is someone to do it with. The same goes for reading. A reading buddy can help you stay on track and hold you more accountable.[345] Thomas Jefferson and John Adams corresponded throughout their adult lives. I am confident they shared their thoughts on what they were reading. At work, my team shares what they are reading.

As I noted before, book clubs are not only great places to get recommendations; they are also great places to share thoughts about books. The common experience is worth a lot. This is especially useful in a work environment. It helps get the entire company moving in the same direction.

Participate in a Reading Challenge

This year, I decided to take part in two reading challenges. The first is through Goodreads, where I committed to reading sixty books in twelve months. The second is the Modern Mrs. Darcy reading challenge, in which participants read twelve books in twelve different categories in twelve months.[346] The challenge has been enjoyable, and has forced me to leave my comfort zone. In the Modern Mrs. Darcy reading challenge, participants were asked to read the following book categories:

- a book published this year
- a book you can finish in a day
- a book you've been meaning to read
- a book recommended by your local librarian or bookseller
- a book you should have read in school
- a book chosen for you by your spouse, partner, sibling, child, or best friend
- a book published before you were born
- a book banned at some point
- a book you'd previously abandoned
- a book you own but have never read
- a book that intimidates you
- a book you've already read at least once

This would be a great workplace challenge. A list of books could be crafted around a specific reading list or topical areas. For example, I work in higher education, and I could develop a list of books around instructional design, gamification, or online learning. For my Air Force brethren, I would challenge them to read the Air Force Chief of Staff reading list.

Wrap Up

Set reading as a priority if you want to read more. I recommend beginning with setting reading goals around which a reading list can be developed. Once a reading list is in place, you can then set time to whittle away at the list. Trimming away distractions and reading "in the margins" will help you achieve your goal.

You can set up all kinds of goals and systems, but if you struggle with reading, it can be a challenge to meet these goals. The next chapter provides strategies for improving reading skills.

CHAPTER SIX

Reading Skills

There are many strategies that can be used to find more time to read as well as develop a reading habit. But this is all for naught if you struggle with reading. Like any skill, the more you work at it, the better you'll become. Reading is no different. Through practice and the application of techniques, you can improve your reading skill, thus becoming a faster reader.

Reading Skills

"Surviving and thriving as a professional today demands two new approaches to the written word. First, it requires a new approach to orchestrating information, by skillfully choosing what to read and what to ignore. Second, it requires a new approach to integrating information, by reading faster and with greater comprehension." —JIMMY CALANO

"The art of reading is the art of adopting the pace the author has set. Some books are fast and some are slow, but no book can be understood if it is taken at the wrong speed." —MARK VAN DOREN

If you want to read more, you may need to improve your reading skills. Improving vocabulary and reading faster are the two essential reading skills. I developed these two skills while at the Air Force Academy Prep School. We had to learn hundreds of new words and practice speed-reading. The faster you read, the more content you can consume. Increasing vocabulary is also essential. Having a weak vocabulary will slow reading. With that in mind, let's begin with a vocabulary lesson.

Vocabulary Building

The importance of having a strong vocabulary was one of the key take-aways I learned at the Air Force Academy Prep School. Daily, we attended vocabulary lessons as part of English classes. We learned hundreds of new words. I am pleased to say many of those words are still part of my daily speech. Learning new vocabulary through regular instruction is one way to build vocabulary, but not the only way. As the Johnson O'Connor Research Foundation notes, we learn new words each day through interaction with media and contact with others.[347] We can speed up our progress with a systematic approach.

Why Build Vocabulary?

A stronger vocabulary will help extract you the exact meaning from what someone is saying or writing. Reading many different types of documents can increase vocabulary and understanding. An increased vocabulary will help with reading and listening. Additionally, it will help with other communication skills such as speaking and writing.

Subvocalizing what is read is natural when reading.[348] Even expert readers subvocalize text, but they do so at a faster speed. By increasing vocabulary, the subvocalization bottleneck can be reduced, thus increasing reading speed.

Unfamiliar words will reduce reading speed. Even though I often read journal articles related to education, I still struggle with certain terms. I am aware that this impacts my reading speed and comprehension.

Malcolm X used his time in jail to build his vocabulary by studying the dictionary page by page.[349] This helped him become an avid reader as well as an influential speaker and leader.

Steps to Building a Vocabulary

There are many strategies for building vocabulary. A reader can pursue each one as an independent exercise or use them in combination. I recommend combining them.

Be Aware of Words

Simply being aware of words is the first step to an increased vocabulary.[350] Rather than pass over unfamiliar words, take time to recognize them and learn about them. Make this a daily practice while reading. Make a note of a word you do not understand from the context. Underline or circle that word to check later. Write the word in the margin and add a definition, or write the word in a vocabulary notebook.

Reading

Reading is one of the easiest ways to build a vocabulary.[351] A reader will see new words in context and can in most cases discern their meanings. Vocabulary will strengthen as the complexity and reading level increases, and will grow as more diverse content is read. For example, reading financial reports will grow vocabulary in one direction, while reading academic journals will grow it in another. Read one article per week for the sole purpose of expanding vocabulary.[352] Finding things you enjoy reading is also important, and may contribute to building a vocabulary.

Maintain a Vocabulary Notebook

Once you've finished a chapter, book, or article, go back and note the definitions for unknown words.[353] Annotate the new words and their definitions in a vocabulary notebook, which can be a physical notebook or a digital file. Many dictionary programs and e-reading applications allow taking notes and highlighting terms and phrases. Many dictionary apps will also provide the proper pronunciation of a new word.[354]

By maintaining a list, you can go back and review the unknown words. You will be surprised by how quickly the list builds over time. Ideally, this list should be portable so it can be pulled out and studied during free time and when not reading.

Expanding upon the vocabulary list idea, keep the list in a spreadsheet with columns. The Johnson O'Connor Research Foundation recommends creating columns dedicated to the "word you want to learn, its part of speech (noun, verb, etc.), its pronunciation, synonyms for the word, its antonyms, its derivation (learning those Greek and Latin roots will help), common meanings of the words, related words, and sentences that illustrate how the word is used."[355]

Keep a Dictionary Handy

When I was in prep school, we each had a dictionary and a thesaurus. I used them throughout my academic career, but less so now. I have moved to digital versions of these two important references. Keep a dictionary readily available, somewhere close to where you regularly read.

When looking up an unfamiliar word, check not only its full definition, but also synonyms and antonyms. Circle or underline unfamiliar words in the dictionary while looking them up. That way, you'll have an opportunity to brush up on unfamiliar words each time you reference the dictionary.

Looking up definitions to words is one of the most useful Google hacks. For example, if I wanted to define "triumvirate," I would type "Define:triumvirate" in the search box.

Word a Day

Many people subscribe to a word-a-day application and have a new word show up on their screens or in their email.[356] Others buy special word-a-day calendars. There are many programs available, with different methods of delivery. Some newspapers also include a word-a-day feature. For example, the *New York Times* has a word of the day column in its printed paper as well as online. The online version also includes a quizzing feature.

The challenge with word-a-day programs, calendars, and columns is making it a habit. The benefits are huge. Learning three new words a day will result in a thousand new words in a year. This systematic increase will help understanding and speed as a reader.

Set Aside Time to Review

Set aside time each day to maintain a word list as well as review the vocabulary list.[357] Rather than studying words during one long review session each week, review during shorter sessions each day. Work on developing a habit of reviewing words. There are programs on the internet that can help you study vocabulary.

Games

Games are a fun way to learn new words. There are solo games or games played with others. Games can be analog or digital. Examples include Scrabble, crossword puzzles, Boggle, anagrams, and word jumble.

Learning Latin Roots

Learning Latin and Greek roots, prefixes, and suffixes for words is one of the strategies I picked up in prep school. This strategy will help understanding the meaning of words as you read them in context.

Vocabulary-Building Books

Vocabulary lessons at the Air Force Academy Prep School centered on books with hundreds of words, definitions, and exercises. The first advantage of vocabulary-building books is they present words generally considered important to know. This is a huge timesaver. Another advantage is they will use the words in several sentences, so you can see the words in different contexts. A third advantage is they usually have exercises that test what is learned, which gives a clear sense of progress.[358] While these books may be challenging, they can help develop vocabulary. Often these books will structure vocabulary lessons around prefixes, roots, and suffixes.[359]

Using Aids While Reading

With smartphones, iPads, and computers at arm's reach, an unfamiliar word can be looked up in the moment of need. A dictionary is always at our disposal. For example, if you're unfamiliar with a location referenced in a book, use Google Maps as a quick way to gain your bearings.

Speed-Reading

Speed reading is another skill I picked up at the Air Force Academy Prep School. We learned various speed-reading techniques and strategies. These techniques helped increase my reading speed to two thousand words per minute at the time.

Leaders should learn how to speed-read. It offers a way to consume more content in less time, thus leading to a competitive advantage in business.

Limitations to Speed-Reading

Although my timed reading speed was two thousand words per minute, there are some who do not believe such speeds are possible due to physiological limitations related to fixation, saccades, and processing.[360] Fixation is the snapshot a reader's eye takes. Saccades are the movements from one fixation to another. The last challenge is the processing the brain must do for each fixation. Thus, very high speeds interfere with comprehension. But low rates of speed allow the brain to wander and affect comprehension. Somewhere in between is a sweet spot where speed is at an optimal level for comprehension. This is often much faster than many people read.

Understanding and training can overcome physiological limitations.[361] Here are a few strategies for overcoming these limitations:[362]

- Reduce the number and duration of fixations.
- Cut regression and backtracking. Do not go back to reread sections.
- Increase the number of words read in one fixation.

Comprehension

Comprehension is another essential reading skill. "Being able to read critically instead of skimming for factoids requires one to assess the words used, the logic of the argument, or the validity of one opinion over another."[363]

As noted above, reading speed affects comprehension. Everyone seems to have a sweet spot for comprehension. Many factors affect comprehension when reading, including the complexity of the material, physiological factors, and subvocalization.

Many speed-reading systems try to cut subvocalization.[364] But research indicates reducing subvocalization also affects comprehension. The narration function of the brain seems to rely on this processing function.

About five hundred words per minute is the fastest one can read and still have adequate comprehension. However, most college-level readers are reading at about two hundred to four hundred words per minute.[365] Doubling reading speed allows someone to consume twice as much information.

Tips for Improving Reading Speed

Breaking habits and focusing on specific reading strategies makes increasing reading speed possible. Here are a few ways to improve your reading speed.

Track Reading Speed

First, determine how many words per minute you read, so that you can measure your improvement. Then you will be able to compare the measurement after using strategies to improve your reading speed.

Here are some basic measurements to take:

Baseline. Before beginning, you must measure your baseline reading speed. Start by calculating the word count of the book being read. Here is a method for calculating a word count:[366]

- Count the number of words in five lines of text, divide the number of words by five, and round the result. For example, 73 words divided by 5 lines equals 14.6. Round this up to 15 words per line.
- Count the number of lines of text on five pages, divide the number of lines by five, and round the result. The result is the average number of lines per page.
- Multiply the average number of lines by the average number of words per line. This yields the average number of words per page.
- Next, read for exactly one minute at normal speed for comprehension. Count the number of lines read and multiply the result by the average word count per line. This is your reading speed in words per minute (WPM).

Words per Minute. Words per minute is the basic speed-reading measurement. WPM is the number of pages read times the number of words per average page divided by the number of minutes spent reading.[367] Speed is not the only factor in play. The reader must also be able to comprehend what is being read.

We had to log reading speed while at prep school. We read articles that had a word count. After reading the article, we noted the time it took and calculated the WPM. This was further adjusted based on a content-comprehension examination.

Be Prepared to Read. Take time to prepare to read when settling in for a reading session. This means ensuring there are note-taking tools at hand, as well as clean glasses or other magnifying devices, if needed. Adjust the size of the print on the screen if using an e-reader. Take a moment to hydrate. All these little things become distractions if not taken into consideration at the outset.

Read Early in the Day. Many people experience increased concentration in the early part of the day, resulting in increased reading speed.[368] Fatigue sets in toward the end of the day, and focusing on material becomes more challenging. Pick a time of day that works best for you and the reading material.

Rank the Reading. Not all reading is the same. Some material you select to read is more important than other pieces. You may have a collection of books or articles that you need to read for work. You may also have books you wish to read for you own development. It is useful to prioritize your reading into different piles from most important to least important. Tackle the most important reading when your mind is the most alert.[369]

Scan Material for Key Points. Conduct an inspectional reading or survey of the book first, an activity known as skimming or scanning. This will help identify what is important to the author. Examine the front and back covers, the table of contents, chapter titles, headings, and subheadings. Also, take time to look at images, tables, and figures. This will help you understand the structure of the book.[370] Reading style and speed needed for comprehension will be easier to gauge. Scanning content can lead to higher comprehension.[371] By first scanning the book or document, a reader can understand what to expect out of a document. This is more applicable to nonfiction.

Avoid Highlighting. If you wish to increase reading speed, avoid highlighting the text.[372] Once you have read a section or chapter, you can go back to take notes or highlight key sections. Highlighting will slow reading and diminish comprehension during the initial read through of the chapter or section. Note that, in a later section, I will contradict this recommendation, as highlighting can be useful for comprehension.

Use a Pointer. Using a pointer to help pace through a page is another strategy I learned at the prep school.[373] This is known as meta-guiding.[374] A finger or pencil can be used to run down the center of a page and guide the eye down the page. This will help pace fixations while reading content. Hold the pen flat on the page so it underlines each line of text as you move down the page.[375] At the prep school, we learned to use a piece of paper or card to underline each line of text so it covered the text not yet read. The reader would read the line above the paper or pen. This strategy will help prevent backtracking while reading.[376]

Another strategy is to have the pen or paper above the line you want to read next so you don't regress or reread material.

Adjust Reading Speed. Reading everything at the same speed is not possible, and you should not attempt to do so. A novel should not be read the same way as a scientific textbook. Vary reading speed to max-imize comprehension. Most novels should be read much quicker than a legal contract.

Use an Application to Practice Speed-Reading. There are many free and paid computer applications that can assist in practicing speed-reading. Some of these applications are standalone programs for a Mac or PC. Others are web-based or part of a browser. Some of these applications allow inserting text while others allow using articles from bookmarking services. Finally, these applications use different methods for presenting text. Some show one word at a time; others use meta-guiding.[377]

Complete a Speed-Reading Course. Taking a speed-reading course is one of the most important methods for increasing speed. The course I took at the prep school helped me. I learned many strategies to read faster. It also provided a dedicated time to practice the skills I learned. President Kennedy had taken a speed-reading course and encouraged his staff to do so as well.

Learning to Speed-Read

Here is a summary of the steps we've looked at to increase speed while reading.[378]

Step 1: Calculate a Reading Baseline. Calculate your reading baseline before using the process described above.

Step 2: Use a Pointer. Use a pointer as a pacing tool while reading. First, practice using the pacer to get used to it. Ferris recommends beginning with a one-second-per-line rate.[379] Practice this a few minutes for a couple of rounds.

Once you're comfortable, increase the speed per line to half a second per line. Repeat this process in three-minute rounds. The key is to focus on the task at hand.

Step 3: Reduce Fixations. Decrease the number of saccades or fixation points per line of text. At the prep school, we spent time trying to read down the center of the page rather than bouncing the eye many times on each line.

Capturing more words per fixation is the first step to reducing the number of fixations.[380] Rather than start on the first word of the line, start on the second or third and end two or three words before the end of the line.

Try to reduce the number of fixations to two fixations per line as you become more comfortable.

Increase the speed at which you read each line once your comfort level rises. Start with one second per line and increase the speed to half a second per line.

Continue to use the pointer as a pacer.

Reading newspaper columns is another way to practice reduced fixations.[381] Try to read each column one line at a time. Use a pacer to help control the speed.

Step 4: Recalculate Reading Speed. Recalculate reading speed by reading for exactly one minute after you become comfortable with your new skills.[382]

Skim and Scan. Not everything in a book is important. There are appropriate times to skim or scan material to get to the important content.[383] This is a technique Theodore Roosevelt used. According to Roosevelt, "The wise thing to do is simply to skip the bosh and twaddle and vulgarity and untruth, and get the benefit out of the rest."[384]

Reading fast has its advantages, especially for consuming more content to help improve one's life. But it comes at a cost. Speed-reading requires more concentration; thus, it can be more tiresome.[385] I recommend using these techniques to increase your reading speed to a level where you can still enjoy what is being read, but not so fast that it's exhausting.

Wrap Up

Business leaders recognize that time is a precious commodity. Individuals should also recognize that they must continuously grow and develop. Reading is a powerful way to gain new knowledge to help improve and grow a business. The faster you can read, the more knowledge you can take in. There are strategies to increase reading speed, but they require practice. A key component to reading faster is developing vocabulary, which will help all other communication skills.

Once you've improved the skills for reading, it's a matter of adapting them to the reading material at hand. Different materials require varying strategies if you want to benefit from a reading session. The next chapter focuses on an active academic reading strategy. This strategy has helped me prepare to read new books with the intent of squeezing the essence from the text.

CHAPTER SEVEN

How to Read a Book

There are strategies that can maximize what we get out of a book. Just like improving reading speed and vocabulary, exploring these methods will reveal the best strategy for getting the most out of a book. The processes do not take long, and they set the stage for the best learning results.

This chapter looks at two methods with similar strategies. The first strategy focuses on Adler and Van Doren's book, *How to Read a Book: The Classic Guide to Intelligent Reading*. The other strategy is one I learned and used at the Air Force Academy Prep School, called SQR3.

Preparing for Active Reading

Before beginning to read a book, you must understand why you are reading the book. What are you hoping to get out of it? The same book can be read for a different purpose and a different meaning will be obtained.

To conduct professional reading, you must read with purpose, which is different from reading for simple enjoyment. For professional reading, a book must be read with the goal of understanding the author's message. I was not fully aware of this until I read Adler and Van Doren's book. They describe in detail how to squeeze the essence out of any book.

Adler and Van Doren describe four levels of reading: elementary, inspectional, analytical, and syntopical.[386] The methods I discuss focus upon the inspectional and analytical levels of reading.

These are active reading methods because the reader is trying to answer four questions:[387]

1. What is the book about?
2. What are the main ideas or arguments of the book?
3. Is the book truthful?
4. What is the significance of what one has read?

A reader cannot simply start on page one and read to the end and expect to understand the point the writer is trying to make. The book must be inspected to get a basic understanding of what the book is going to cover. Adler and Van Doren have labeled this method "inspectional reading."[388]

Inspectional Reading

A reader can conduct an inspectional reading in two parts: systematic skimming (pre-reading) and superficial reading.[389]

Preview the book to determine its purpose. There are six steps:[390]

1. Examine the title page and read the preface. What type of book is it?

2. Examine the table of contents. What topics are being covered?

3. Examine the index. What terms do you recognize? Which ones are unfamiliar?

4. Read the publisher's comments on the dust jacket. The dust jacket may provide more insight into the purpose of the book.

5. Read chapter summaries.

6. Thumb through the book and read various passages. This provides a feel of the writing.

This first reading will help you understand the type of book being read and its intended purpose. After that, conduct a superficial reading. The authors recommend making a quick read through the entire book without pausing to look up words, take notes, or reference other resources to gain clarity.[391] "In tackling a difficult book for the first time, read it through without ever stopping to look up or ponder the things you do not understand right away."[392]

By conducting this superficial reading, a reader can "hear" the writer's message uninterrupted. The whole becomes more understandable even if 50 percent escapes the reader during this first reading. The book can be read in much more in depth during the second reading. Remember, a superficial reading should be a fast, uninterrupted read.

Analytical Reading

Analytical reading is studying and thoroughly reading a book. Adler and Van Doren have a checklist of fifteen rules they suggest working through. I apply a small subset of these rules.

As Adler and Van Doren outline, you want to conduct this analytical reading in three phases.[393]

First determine what the book is about. This means classifying the book based on its subject matter. For example, you may want to classify it as nonfiction or fiction. It may be historical or science fiction. You could further classify it such as World War II or post-apocalyptic. You should be able provide a brief description of the book in its entirety. If it is nonfiction, you should be able to identify the problem the author is trying to solve.[394]

The second phase of analytical reading to gain a full understanding of the author's meaning.[395] During this phase you will actively take notes in the book. There are a number of points that you will be focusing on. You will want to identify the author's keywords and concepts. Make it a point to circle or underline these key points. Strive to reconstruct the author's outline to identify the author's arguments. In the end, you want to see if the author provided a solution to the problem they identified.

The final phase is perhaps the most challenging and it must be completed after the first two phases are completed. During this final phase of analytical reading, you are looking for opportunities for criticism.[396] Specifically, you are identifying where the author is misinformed, has faulty logic, or fails to adequately address the arguments set forth in the book.

I can't say I follow all these rules. Also, I do not write down the replies to each of these rules. But I do use most of them when reading a book, usually mentally. For example, I classify the books I read such as technical, historical, business, leadership, and so on. After an inspectional or analytical read, I can state what the book is about and the main points the author is trying to make. While I may not write a formal outline, I do try to outline the book in my head. I also try to determine the problems the author has dealt with and the solutions recommended.

Reading *How to Read a Book: The Classic Guide to Intelligent Reading* has caused me to reexamine how I read books. If you do a lot of reading, I recommend this book. It will improve how the way you absorb professional reading material. The methods described will help you read at a deeper level.

SQR3

SQR3 or SQ3R is another analytical reading method. I learned this while at the Air Force Academy Preparatory School. SQR3 is a method used to study a book or textbook in preparation for a test and is also an active form of reading. There are five parts: survey or scan, question, read, recite, and review.

Survey. The layout of the book is discerned when surveying a book. This means front and back covers are examined, as well as the table of contents, chapter titles, headings, and subheadings. The index, images, charts, maps, introductions, and summaries are also studied. This helps identify what was important to the author.

Question. Next, question the book. In this step, turn titles, headings, subheadings, keywords, and key phrases into questions. For example, for this section, one could write "What is SQR3?" and "What is questioning in regards to SQR3?" Write these questions on notecards or in an analog or digital notebook.

While taking notes, keep an eye out for formulas, keywords or bolded words, and other emphasized aspects of the book.[397] These elements should help guide your questions and note-taking.

Read. With questions in hand, read the book. When you read the book, your intent should be to answer the questions. Look for clues in the opening paragraphs and opening sentences of each paragraph. You can also find clues at the ends of chapters, in picture captions, and near keywords. You should be taking notes during this phase. First read the section or paragraph fully before taking notes, so the main points are captured.[398] Additionally, you can add extra questions to your question bank. Move to the recite step when completing a chapter. Do this before advancing to the next chapter to ensure you understand the concepts.

If you're reading as part of a course, use this time to write down questions to ask in class.[399] You may also want to consider highlighting specific portions of the reading assignment, so you can refer to them during class discussions.

When you finish a chapter, take time to summarize what you read. Quite often, there is space at the end of a chapter to write this summary, or you can write the summary in your digital notes. You can find more about note-taking in the note-taking chapter.

Recite. In the recite step, you're going to read the questions you had written down and try to discern the answers. If you have difficulty answering the question, go back to the book, find the answer, and summarize the points. You can also make annotations in the book to emphasize key points.

Review. The final step is review. First, review any notes you've written. Next, work through questions written on the notecards and try to answer them. If you come up with incorrect answers, take more notes to help you clarify the concept and remember the material. Repeat this process as often as necessary.

More SQR3 Notes. In "Reading a Textbook for True Understanding," the authors offer tips for successful academic reading.[400] The first tip focuses on pacing. They recommend calculating the time needed for a reading assignment by multiplying the number of pages by five minutes. They don't advise completing a reading assignment in one sitting. Rather, they recommend breaking the reading into ten-page chunks.

Wrap Up

This chapter offered strategies to better read a book. Previewing the material to understand what you're going to read will increase the likelihood of getting more out of the book. Other strategies like the SQR3 will help if you're reading for an academic setting. Questioning can move you from a passive to an active reader. Take a moment to look ahead as you grab your next book to get a feel for what you will read.

Reading is not a passive activity. When you read, you should be actively taking notes. The next chapter explores note-taking as it applies to reading.

CHAPTER EIGHT

Note-Taking

"I used to always read with a pen in my hand, as if the author and I were in a conversation." —TARA BRAY SMITH

Now that you have learned more about how to read a book and the questions you should be asking in preparation, it is time to learn about note-taking as it applies to reading. I am going to encourage you to have a dialogue with your book, in the book.

Write in a book? How dare you! Well, I dare you. A reader enters a deep dialogue with the author by adding notes while reading. You have an opportunity to connect to prior experiences and to reference previous books. The book will never be the same and neither will the reader—each changes for the better. Annotations leave a part of an individual in the quest for knowledge.

This chapter explores taking notes in physical and digital books and shows digital and paper-based note-taking tools.

Taking Notes in Books

Throughout history, readers have scribbled notes in books while reading. They have highlighted passages they thought important. They have expressed agreements and disagreements with authors. They have also tied their knowledge together with elaborate referencing systems. Marginalia is the term for marking in the margins of books. In previous chapters, it has been documented that speed-reading and consuming more books per year has many advantages. I explored some techniques and encouraged you to increase the pace with which you read effectively. Taking notes and learning these skills are not meant to conflict with reading faster. Logically, if you read faster while taking notes, you would still increase your consumption of written works within a given period of time. Depending on the material and purpose for reading a particular selection, note-taking will vary in its intensity.

Note-Taking in Physical Books

I begin with a simple strategy for marking up a physical book. As I conduct an analytical reading, I make a mark in the margin to note a key idea or concept. This is a vertical line indicating the number of sentences or lines and an asterisk. I use many asterisks if the information is essential. Additionally, if the material generates a thought or association with other material, I make a small note in the margin of the book. I may underline keywords, new words, and phrases I want to remember or explore later.

Some take offense to taking notes in a book. I can respect that. There are many ways to take notes, and many do not require defacing a book. Yet, for me, I want to pay the highest respect to the author by having a conversation with him or her on the pages.

Other Marking Strategies

Every reader has his or her own way of taking notes. Here are strategies others have shared.

One reader adds comments to margins as he questions the author.[401] At the end of each chapter, he summarizes the chapter with bullet notes. Another offers an indexing method for summarizing books.[402] I have included it below.

Highlighters and Colored Pens

While I prefer to mark my books with a pen, others prefer a highlighter. I used to use a highlighter, but for some reason I abandoned this method. Some use a combination of highlighters and pens, highlighting a few key phrases and then going back to write notes as a guide.[403] Others recommend against using markers and suggest using colored pens to write in the book.[404] You can use different colors to highlight key points, quotes, and ideas.[405]

Coding

A note taker can create codes to help mark up a text.[406] Here are some recommended codes:

- Asterisk or star for topic sentences.
- Question marks for disagreement.
- Exclamation marks for agreement.
- Circling unfamiliar terms or phrases.
- Arrows to connect related thoughts.
- Underline interesting thoughts.

Some readers note specific phrases or language they like. For example, you might use "PH" to note a phrase and "BL" for "beautiful language."[407] Fighting the urge to mark everything in the book is one of the more difficult skills to develop. Experienced readers suggest emphasizing no more than 20 percent of what is read.[408] This allows important points to shine through. This is something I struggle with, although I am making a conscious effort to control it.

Post-it Notes

Some people prefer to jot notes and page numbers on Post-it notes. They then affix the Post-it notes to the various pages of the book.[409] Post-it notes can be rearranged to suit the reader's needs after finishing reading. A reader can upload and organize the notes based on the color of the Post-it note using Evernote's Post-it feature. For example, one color could be used for quotes and another for further research.

Post-it notes can be used as bookmarks to help locate information in a book.[410] For example, you can write on the exposed part of the Post-it note to help identify key sections. Using editing arrow flags is an alternative to Post-it notes.[411] I only used arrow flags once to mark a book—one I had checked out of a library. While it served its purpose, I prefer to buy the book and annotate in the margins.

Mind Map

Other readers capture a mind map or concept map of the key points of books. A mind map is a diagram of the structure of a concept using lines and nodes to reflect a relationship. You can then store the finished mind map next to the first page of the book.[412] Mind maps are great ways to visualize a book's structure.

Extra Note-Taking Strategies for Fiction

Reading and note-taking are different for fiction and nonfiction. Many of the same note-taking ideas apply, such as marking in the book, but there are nuances.

"In literary criticism, the term close reading describes the careful, sustained interpretation of a brief passage of a text. A close reading emphasizes the single and the particular over the general, effected by close attention to individual words, the syntax, and the order in which the sentences unfold ideas, as the reader scans the line of text."[413]

Cornell College offers suggestions for a close reading of fictional works. These suggestions focus on an academic environment, but will work for anyone who hopes to gain wisdom from what they read.

Here are some tips from Cornell College:[414]

- Completely read a few paragraphs before taking notes. You will better understand the essence of what is read before interacting with the material.
- Look for patterns in content as well as connections to previous material.
- After marking up the book, use note cards to capture information about characters, themes, arguments, settings, descriptions, imagery, grammar patterns, semantics, and foreshadowing.
- When capturing notes about character behavior or development, be specific. Annotate a descriptive phrase along with a page number so that you can find the reference again.[415]

Indexing Books

The article "A Simple Guide to Indexing the Books You Read for Evernote" provides a wonderful way to index books one reads.[416] First, create an index of important findings on a blank page next to the inside of the cover of the book. Next, photograph the index and save it to your Evernote notebook. You will then be able to locate a book you need by searching Evernote.

Here are some tips for this indexing method:

- Use a page that is blank on both sides for the indexing page.
- Note important quotes, lists, points, and so on by annotating the page and making a short reference on the index page.
- If a quote is especially noteworthy, write it on the index page.
- Handwriting must be neat for Evernote to find the notes.
- Use a notebook or tag to organize book indexes.

Another strategy is to capture key points as bullets at the end of each chapter.[417] Try to envision how you will apply what you've learned. When you've finished reading and note-taking, you can add annotations to your commonplace book. I describe commonplace books in more detail below.

When taking notes, write them in your own words. This will help you engage with the material better than simply copying and pasting passages. Use copy and paste only for direct quotes. Identify if direct quotes are taken.

Developing Glossaries

As an extension of building a vocabulary list, create a separate sheet of unfamiliar terms that can be updated over time.[418] Define these terms in your own words. If you're stuck for a definition, I recommend the Oxford Dictionary (https://en.oxforddictionaries.com/).

Note-Taking in Digital Books

I, like many others, have started to read more on devices such as the Kindle or Nook. According to Pew Internet, "A fifth of American adults have read an e-book in the past year and the number of e-book readers grew after a major increase in ownership of e-book reading devices and tablet computers during the holiday gift-giving season."[419] I have 102 books on my iPad, with about 10 books I am waiting to read. As I read a book, I highlight the chapter number and heading for later reference and highlight important or key ideas. My highlights include main ideas and concepts, references to other books I may want to read, and keywords and phrases. I also use Kindle's note feature and type in notes or ideas as they come to me while reading.

When I first started to read e-books, the greatest obstacle was getting notes from the e-book to Zotero, a citation and note-management program. Zotero has been my primary research tool. For a period of time, the Kindle was my professional reading method of choice because I had worked out a solution to transfer notes. Unfortunately, Amazon has changed their algorithm, and I am again looking for a smooth process. I have been exploring Evernote as a repository for the notes I am currently taking on my Kindle. Being able to digitize my notes has made gathering notes and quotes much faster. This allows me to focus on writing, research, and creating, instead of transcribing. I will be purchasing more e-books in the future because of the ability to copy digital notes.

Although I am a fan of e-books, I must agree with current research, which indicates that taking notes for digital books can be more challenging and interfere with understanding.[420] There is something powerful for learning when you can underline phrases and words, write in the margins, and circle unknown words. Nonetheless, I still enjoy reading books on my Kindle.

Managing Notes Once Taken

While it is important to take notes while reading, it is also important to use the notes in a meaningful way after the fact. Notes must retrievable and available for use in relation to other notes to have the most benefit. I have found it useful to keep my notes in a central data repository. Having a system, whether paper-based or digital, for easy retrieval is important. My digital tools of choice are Zotero and Evernote. With each tool, I can search across all the notes I have created to focus on a single topic. No matter how I consume a book, I also have a small notebook available to take notes as I read or hear them. Additionally, I capture quick notes using Evernote's audio-recording features. Let's explore a few digital tools and methods for organizing notes.

Digital Tools to Capture a Note

There are countless digital tools for taking notes. Digital tools are effective for capturing, identifying, remembering, and recalling information.[421] Besides Zotero and Evernote, Google Docs and Microsoft Word are options.

Digitizing Notes

When capturing notes, create a record of the book or article, including title, author, publishing date, and publisher information. For basic bibliographical information, I recommend using the latest APA (American Psychological Association), MLA (Modern Language Association), or Chicago Manual of Style guide. One should also be able to add tags to help with finding related notes. Here are the tools and processes I use.

Zotero. Zotero is not only helpful with note-taking; it is also a powerful tool for conducting research. Zotero is a citation-management system, which allows for tagging, searching, note-taking, collecting, and sharing. I started using Zotero a couple of years ago to support my doctoral program. It was a great place to collect and organize the notes for my dissertation. Now I also use Zotero to collect notes on everything I read. These notes have been useful when I need to support a position, write a blog post, or in many other writing projects. Zotero is a database of resources. It houses these resource references in a main library. The main library may consist of book references, journal articles, news stories, reports, conferences, and so on. These references can be organized into collections. For example, a dissertation chapter, journal article, or business report can be created. You can also share libraries with others. This also includes associated notes and tags. This is a great way to cowrite an article or book.

The power of Zotero lies in its search engine. Articles can be found with a simple search. The search engine will hunt through all parts of a reference to include the bibliography information, notes, tags, and indexed PDFs. You can drill down and identify references related to a specific tag, and can also sort references based on many options, including title, creator, author, date, publisher, and call number.

I have found Zotero invaluable to my reading and writing process. I used a combination of Scrivener, Zotero, and Evernote to write this book.

Evernote. Evernote is also another great place to capture digital notes. You can type in notes, take a picture of handwritten notes, or copy and paste from Kindle highlights. Evernote has a powerful camera-and-search combination. If you find something particularly interesting on a Kindle page, you can capture a screenshot on your iPad or cell phone and upload it to Evernote. Evernote has the capability to search through images for specific words, and will highlight the word on the image. Keep in mind that the highlights are actual quotes from the book. Once the notes are uploaded, you can add tags and other notes to help locate this valuable information later.

Some readers will capture the main arguments in Evernote, along with questions they still want answered. One reader I know uses a pen to place a dot next to a key point or quote in a book and goes back to capture the note in Evernote. Many people use Evernote in the way people once used commonplace books. However, commonplace books are usually limited to paper and ink. Evernote can capture much more.

With Evernote, pictures of written notes can be taken and virtually accessed anywhere. You can thus enjoy the power of the handwritten note as well as the digital accessibility. Research indicates that writing notes strengthens understanding and critical thinking compared to typing a note.[422]

Google Docs. Some prefer to capture their notes in Google documents. Google can be central to your information center.[423] Because Google provides a host of applications in addition to Google Docs such as Gmail, Google Calendar, spreadsheets, slide presentations, to-do lists, document storage, and more, it is a powerful ecosystem in which to capture your notes.

Google documents can be accessed from all devices, thus making it an easily accessed tool. I like Google documents as a collaboration tool. I can share documents I have written and can cowrite documents in real time with others.

Other Word Processors. Other word processors, such as Microsoft Word, can record notes. You can keep an open file while reading to capture key points and quotes. Because they are digital, files can be found through computer searches.

Paper-Based Note-Taking Systems

Many readers are more comfortable using a paper-based system to organize notes. You can develop a system using folders, binders, notebooks, or note cards, in which you can quickly find information.

I used analog systems for many years, but after a couple of household moves, I found the footprint of the analog systems too large and taxing. I digitized thousands of pages of notes to PDF documents and put them into Evernote. I can now find notes as well as share them with others.

Common Paper-Based Systems

Whatever the system, it must work for the system's owner. Here are some paper-based and analog systems to experiment with.

Folders. Folders are useful for combining information on like items. A filing system maintains and organizes folders. Folders can be used to organize digital artifacts on a computer. A referencing system can combine paper and digital systems.

Binders. Ringed binders are also an effective way to maintain notes.

Binders can be created for different topics, moments in time, or many other reasons. Folders can further subdivide binders.

Notebooks. Notebooks can also be great tools to save notes. A couple of years ago, I adopted bullet journaling after reading about it. It has changed how I capture much of what I do in life. I am using it to capture ideas, things to do, and lists of books and applications. I have it with me wherever I go. However, though I use it to capture the proceedings of a conference, I don't use it to capture my reading notes. Many people do use a notebook to capture reading notes.

Here are two common notebook strategies to consider.

Commonplace Book

"In an earlier time, books were expensive. You might have been able to borrow a given book for a short time and then have to return it. That's one reason why the commonplace book was developed."[424]

"A commonplace book is a central resource or depository for ideas, quotes, anecdotes, observations and information you come across during your life and didactic pursuits. The purpose of the book is to record and organize these gems for later use in your life, in your business, in your writing, speaking or whatever it is that you do."[425]

Many famous people, past and present, have kept commonplace books. Writers use them to collect ideas for stories or scripts. Politicians use them to help craft policies or speeches. Business leaders use them to save ideas for new business ventures. Ordinary people throughout history also used commonplace books to save worthwhile ideas. Commonplace books were very much in vogue with intellectuals in the seventeenth and eighteenth centuries.[426] Because of the invention of the printing press, there was suddenly information overload.

These intellectuals used commonplace books to help manage this overload. They captured meaningful wisdom in their books.

"It may seem an esoteric practice, but commonplace has re-emerged among digital explorers as a modern solution to information overload. Like letterpress, typewriters, and writing by hand, a new creative class of authors and knowledge workers are employing commonplace as a way to find deeper connections to their work and life."[427]

Commonplace books may or may not have some type of organization; it is up to the owner of the book. While commonplace books are often paper-based notebooks, they may also be digital. They should be a convenient method for collecting wisdom captured from reading or life in general.

Some advocate for paper-based notebooks over digital.[428] With paper-based systems, there is a greater chance that you will discover a long-lost note while perusing a connection.

Using a Commonplace Book While Reading

The following are strategies for using a commonplace journal:[429]

- Read widely. You never know where a great idea will come from. Read both nonfiction and fiction. Also, read outside of your niche or comfort zone.
- Strive to squeeze the essence and wisdom from a book. Don't consume only the facts.
- Only capture the best ideas, quotes, and concepts in a commonplace book. Don't fill the notebook with everything. Take time to capture the best. Consider waiting a week or two before beginning to transfer the notes to your commonplace book. This will allow the most important concepts to percolate to the top.

- Don't let books pile up before transferring notes.
- Put commonplace books to use. Don't just make deposits in the commonplace book; share the contents with others.
- Commonplace books are a lifetime pursuit, and can capture a snapshot of a person's life. Over time, this will help tell your story. If you don't have a commonplace book, start now.

Harvard University Library's Open Collections Program has a collection of digitized commonplace books from the seventeenth century to the present. It is fascinating to see what others found important as they read.

Bullet Journal

The bullet journal is a variation of the commonplace book. I see each of these having different purposes. The bullet journal idea originated with Ryder Carroll. The bullet journal focuses on keeping one's life in order and on track, but it can also be used to capture inspiration. I will note something I find especially noteworthy in the book, as well as make an annotation in my bullet journal.

Bullet journals are multipurpose documents that track what you're reading and what you're discovering while reading. Many people recommend creating a separate bullet journal dedicated to reading.

I use a Moleskine notebook, but there are many brands out there. I keep a Moleskine bullet journal in my back pocket and capture notes and tasks wherever I may be.

Elements of a Bullet Journal

Being flexible to user needs is one of the most important things about bullet journaling. It can be used for to-do lists or to track ideas and thoughts. Here are the basic elements of a bullet journal.[430]

- Page numbers. Each page has a page number.
- Page titles. Each page has a page title.
- Index. There is an index at the beginning of a book. The index helps you locate specific pages in the journal.
- Events, Tasks, and Notes. The main entries in the journal are bullets, which may be events, tasks, or notes.
- Signifiers. Each bullet will have a special symbol or signifier to show the type of item.

The type of bullet journal created will dictate the modules to include. Each bullet journal should include an index to locate specific items in the journal. My bullet journal index lists specific monthly task listings, book wish lists, application wish lists, and much more.

You may want to include a future log, a monthly log, and a daily log.[431] The future log tracks tasks or events that will occur, but that are not yet in progress. The monthly log is a quick calendar listing events and tasks scheduled for the month. The daily log records events, tasks, or notes.

Using a Bullet Journal to Track Reading

Those who use a bullet journal for managing their reading swear by it. Here are ideas to manage reading using a bullet journal.

Book Wish List. At a very basic level, you can maintain a list of books you want to read. When I hear about a book on a podcast, or if I read about one, I will pull out my bullet journal and add it to my book list. You can check off a book when you buy it. You may also want to state if the book is an e-book, audiobook, or physical book.

Monthly To-Read List. At the beginning of the month, create a section to identify books that you wish to read.[432] Once it's read, mark off the book in bullet journal style. Place an "X" through the bullet point. If a large to-read list makes you jittery, break it down into smaller, weekly reading lists.[433]

Library Books/Bookstore. Create a book list in your bullet journal daily log before going to a library.[434] The convenient list makes it easy to remember which books to pick up. You can also make notes about the availability of the book, reminding you to pick it up later if necessary. This strategy also works before going to a bookstore.

Book Series. Create a special list in your bullet journal if you're reading a series of books or tracking a list of books for a specific author.[435] Consider putting together an authors list.

Reading Statistics. Earlier, I talked about the importance of setting goals and keeping track of metrics. Some of the items a reader could track with a bullet journal include book title, genre, author gender, number of pages, rating, publishing year, book type (fiction/nonfiction), and start and finish dates.[436]

Reading Goals. Some people dedicate a page or part of a page to identify a reading goal. Some create a matrix of squares they color in as they complete a book. Others create a series of bullets to be X'ed out. This collection of reading goals should stand on its own page. The Modern Mrs. Darcy Reading Challenge is a great example of a reading goal. If waiting to check off a book takes too long, create a page listing the chapters of the book. Check off the chapters as you work through them.

Listing Books Read. Within the monthly log, track the different books read.

Capturing Reading Notes. You can dedicate one or more pages to the notes you take for a specific book. I would first follow the ideas for note-taking listed earlier, and then transfer the notes to the bullet journal.

Other Bullet Journal Considerations

- Give lists ample pages to expand.
- Keep side-by-side pages for books to read and books read.

There are many creative ways to show off lists and goals. I encourage you to Google "bullet journal" and read.

Note Cards. Note cards are a useful tool for arranging notes on a specific topic. Some individuals swear by note cards and would not use another system. Note cards may be used to capture notes for books or blog posts that are being written, or you can rearrange the cards for a writing project. President Reagan used note cards to capture quotes, jokes, and issues of the day.[437] They can also be used to capture lifelong ideas.

Here are strategies for a note card system:[438]

- Build a note card deck for each project.

- Use 4x6 note cards.
- Complete a note card for each unique idea, quote, thought, or concept. The thought might consist of just one word.
- Write a category in the upper right-hand corner on each card. This category should reflect the point in the project: introduction, productivity, and so on.
- Color-code the cards if doing so helps with organization.
- Ensure a captured note is accurate, and know where the information came from.
- State if there is more on the back of a card.

One reader collects his notes by first making written notes in the book and, after a couple of weeks, transfers his notes to note cards.[439] This typically takes twenty to thirty cards per book. "Waiting helps you separate the wheat from the chaff. I promise that many of the pages you marked will not seem too important or noteworthy when you return to them."[440]

I used the note card system when writing a paper about the rumored death of Sir Paul McCartney for a class at the Air Force Prep School. The system worked quite well. I used three different levels of colors to organize the cards. One color represented a major outline point, the second color the first level of sub-point, and the third color the second level of sub-point.

When using a note card system, ideas may stick longer because it is paper-based and forces one to handle each card many times while exploring ideas. Revisiting old cards is a reminder of long-lost lessons. If you're looking for a digital version of note cards, a program like Scrivener may be useful.

Combining Note-Taking Systems

The best note-taking system is one that works. My system is a combination of paper-based and digital note-taking. I use a bullet journal for everyday events and tasks. When I finish with a month of notes, I photograph the pages to Evernote, where I can search notes. I will take notes in the books I am reading, whether they are paper-based or digital, and later move the notes to a program like Zotero, where I can use them for research.

The ability to later use the notes is the key to a great note-taking system. Adjust the system if you cannot do this.

Wrap Up

"I have found that a well-marked book, becomes more like a treasured friend—one that you enjoy seeing again and again. It becomes much more enjoyable than a sterile copy that comes straight from the bookstore. Don't be afraid to mark up the books that you love."[441]

—BERT WEBB

If you've marked up a book, when you reread that book, you will start in a different place, in a different relationship. It will be a familiar conversation—one in which you can pick up where you left off.

There are a number of effective ways to take notes. Writing directly on the pages and margins of books allows immediate, personal interactions with the text. Digital programs are available to record a variety of types of information with the benefits of easy access and organization of the notes. Other methods, such as note cards, commonplace books, and bullet journals are also useful. A combination of these methods may be developed to satisfy individual needs.

The ultimate goal of reading is to help improve the world around you. In the next chapter, you will learn about two similar strategies that I use: Seek-Sense-Share and Invest-Learn-Teach.

CHAPTER NINE

Reading Strategies

So far, we have explored why one would want to develop a reading habit, how to develop reading skills, how to read a book, and how to take notes on what an individual reads. This chapter focuses on strategies to find new material, develop an understanding of that material, and share what you learn with others.

I first learned about Seek-Sense-Share from Harold Jarche, a keynote speaker at a conference I attended. He helps businesses improve by changing their learning strategies. More recently, I learned about Ray Higdon's Invest-Learn-Teach framework by listening to *Entrepreneur on Fire*.

Each concept stresses seeking, learning, or making sense of information, and then taking time to teach others through unfettered sharing. I have been eager to learn new things for as long as I can remember and love helping others expand their knowledge. I will start with Seek-Sense-Share, since I am more familiar with it.

Seek-Sense-Share

Seek

In March 2014, at a conference I attended, Harold Jarche encouraged participants to share their personal knowledge-management routine. I thought it was a useful exercise to think about how I work through the framework.

My eyes and ears on the world are the Seek element. For me, seeking is about pulling in new information. The information I curate and consume focuses on areas of interest or problems I am trying to solve. It may also be information I am seeking for another person's problem. Keeping an eye out for new information is a rapid process. I scan article titles for something interesting. If I spot something, I will then open it, read it, and decide whether it's worth keeping. While some sense-making occurs, this step is all about curation.

Reading is a key tool for this stage. I will read a myriad of different content of various lengths and complexities. Each requires a different reading style. Some artifacts only require a simple scan, while others require an in-depth read supported by note-taking. When I am conducting an in-depth study of a topic, I will read a series of books on the topic.

Seeking Tools

Seeking is part of my daily routine. I review a number of input feeds, many of which are part of my morning in-processing routine. Here is what I review:

Email. Email is the primary method for sharing information in my job and is on my in-processing list. I may receive an email that has new information worthy of curating.

E-newsletters. I subscribe to many e-newsletters, most of which focus on social media, instructional design, instructional technology, or some other aspect of using technology in education.

Paper.li. While I have three Twitter accounts, I often aggregate the feeds into unique lists or queries. I use these Twitter lists and queries in a collection of daily or weekly Paper.li newsletters. This simplifies the process of reviewing the newsletters for interesting articles.

LinkedIn, Facebook, and Google Plus. LinkedIn, Facebook, and Google Plus are my go-to social media sites. With LinkedIn, I rely on the email messages I receive from the different groups to which I belong. I visit Facebook and Google Plus each day to see what is interesting and new. Facebook is about family and friends, while Google Plus provides a more professional feed. I will often curate something new or share it immediately.

RSS Feeds and Podcasts. I have more than one hundred RSS feeds loaded in my Feedly for review. Feedly is an RSS feed aggregator. It allows you to stream posts from multiple sources into one convenient place for reading. I review these articles for interesting new content. My feeds focus on areas of interest such as informal learning, gamification, and e-learning. I am amazed and humbled by what I read from many prolific writers.

Podcasts. Podcasts are new to my routine. I usually compile a collection of podcast feeds and go for a ride or walk my dogs while listening to them. I have a notebook to capture new ideas as I hear them.

Webinars, MOOCs, Online Courses, and Virtual Meetings. These four online learning events also help feed my learning appetite. I watch Webinars to learn about new ideas. When I can, I also take part in Massive Open Online Courses (MOOCs). My completion rate is not as high as I would like, but at least I am jumping into the fray. When I am teaching an online course, I tap into the knowledge and expertise of the learners in the class. In fact, I might learn more from teaching the courses than they do as students. I also learn a great deal from the various virtual meetings I attend with professional colleagues.

Books and Magazines. Magazines and books are the cornerstone of my lifelong learning process. I receive a few professional magazines each month, but books are my main feed. I buy books for my Kindle as well as stock up on books as I attend conferences. Many of the top CEOs have placed a strong emphasis on reading. They believe reading has helped them be productive and innovative.

I will consume new content in print or on a digital device (computer, iPad, smartphone), depending upon what I am consuming. Some devices are better suited for consumption than others. I will go into more detail on this in subsequent chapters.

I discover new books to read through many different avenues: Goodreads recommendations, podcast recommendations, and searches to solve problems.

That is how I go about seeking information to keep me moving forward. What do you do to pull in new information? How do you stay current?

Sense

Sense is the second component of Seek-Sense-Share. Sense is about understanding what one curates and consumes. Sense-making should be a regular process during which you feed new information through a personal experience filter to develop new knowledge or reinforce what you already know. Also, sense-making is what we put into practice.

For me, the process of sense-making is necessary before I share information with others. My responsibility in my various roles is to help me find and distribute new content to help others excel. Sense-making is a key part of this process because I must first understand the content. I must then know how the new knowledge will benefit others before I can share. Sense-making may occur while I am seeking information, or it may be a distinct function as I am getting ready to share what I have learned with others.

Sense-Making Tools

Here are the tools I use as part of my sense-making:

Blogs. My blogs are the centerpiece of my sense-making. My first blog started as an exercise for a class I took with Michael Day, now professor emeritus of the University of Wyoming. My blog has evolved into a place where I reflect upon and share what I learn. I document my learning journey in my personal blog. The other two blogs are tools where I share what I have discovered with specific audiences.

Zotero. As mentioned earlier, I write my notes into Zotero while participating in professional reading. I now have countless articles and books listed in Zotero with my notes. I can filter and search this resource to craft new understanding on a topic. It was indispensable to my dissertation-writing process. Kindle and Zotero make a great note-capture combination. Zotero is specifically suited to citation management.

Evernote. If I am watching a Webinar, attending a presentation, or listening to a podcast, I will usually have Evernote open to capture my notes. I can take notes using text, audio, documents, and images. It is my electronic brain. If I am taking a note in a notebook, I will photograph the page and save it to Evernote, where I can later search for it. I have scanned into Evernote notes I have taken earlier in my life, so I can reference them. Evernote is often my starting point for note-taking. I will typically move articles I collected in Evernote to Zotero if I am working on a more formal writing project, such as a book or an article. Evernote is so versatile I cannot imagine working without it.

Diigo. If capturing a web-based resource, I will often save it to Diigo. I have over ten thousand sites saved, and have tagged them for easy retrieval. I reference my collections as I write blog posts or put presentations together. If someone asks me for references on a topic, I will generally give them a Diigo tag link related to their topic.

Presentation Creating. Creating a presentation is very much a sense-making process. I must organize the material in a way that makes sense to me and others. Often when working through the process of building a presentation, I will develop some new insight into the problem I am addressing. I share my presentations to Slideshare for the benefit of others.

Book Writing. Finally, writing this book has been an exercise of sense-making. The entire process has been a learning experience that has caused me to explore my understanding of reading in much more depth.

That is how I go about making sense of this changing world. What do you do to make sense of your part of the world?

Share

While each element is critical to this framework, I am an especially big fan of the Share element. Sharing is an opportunity to add to the world knowledge base with an interpretation of what one has learned. Sharing helps others develop, with a diffusion of lessons and ideas learned.

Individual development is the focus of the Seek and Sense elements. However, the Share element not only helps individual development, but also organizational and community development. Learning is about dialogue; dialogue either with content or with others. By sharing content, a door is opened to dialogue and learning with those in a network. Over time, others actually begin to better understand you as an individual through what you share. They come to learn your likes, dislikes, interests, and motivations. They will in turn share relevant content with you.

As Jarche talked about sharing information back out to the world, he cautioned that we have a responsibility to add value to what we shared. Don't share for the sake of sharing—make a difference by helping connect the dots.

Sharing Tools

My sharing tools are rather limited, and I don't always go the extra step to add value as I should, although I have improved. I use sharing as an opportunity to work out loud. I reply to questions and share lessons I

149

learn with the public, using blogs and videos when I work out loud. Jarche and Hart also discussed the concept of working out loud at the National Extension Conference I had attended.

Here is a list of tools I use to share what I have learned:

Blogs. My blogs are my primary tools for sharing. What once was a school project has developed into a means for me to document my learning journey. I also use blogs to share book reviews I write. For each book I read, I try to write a quick book review to reflect upon what I read. I often pull in one or two new ideas into my practices. Book reviews are also an important strategy in which employees take part. While I may not have my team write book reviews, I do encourage them to share what they are reading and how it helps the team perform better. I also use my blogs to share new ideas on how to use technology in support of learning or teaching. Finally, I use blogs as a vehicle to answer questions I receive. This is another idea I adopted from Jarche.

When I create a blog post, automation sends it to Google Plus, Facebook, Twitter, Tumblr, and LinkedIn. If you have limited time, this is an efficient way to share to many audiences.

Email. Email is another tool for sharing. But I do not actually share much through email. If I do, I usually share a link to a blog post. In other cases, I may share a specific article with an individual or small group, if it applies to them. This is a strategy I picked up from Keith Ferrazzi's book *Never Eat Alone*.

YouTube. YouTube is my platform of choice if I want to show how to do something. I will create a video with Camtasia or YouTube Live and share through YouTube. My YouTube channel has 350 videos arranged into various playlists. Some of these playlists also contain videos created by others (there is no sense in reinventing the wheel). Very often, I will embed a video into a blog post or place in a course.

Twitter. I share a lot through Twitter. I manage three Twitter accounts: a personal account, a business account, and a work account. I automate much of what I share. A blog post or Paper.li newsletter may generate the tweet. In other cases, I will share a new article that others would enjoy. Another way I share tweets is with lists and search queries organized in Paper.li.

Paper.li. Paper.li aggregates articles based on a search query, a Twitter list, or other list. Individuals can subscribe to the newsletter, and it will arrive in their email inbox. Additionally, Paper.li will send out a tweet for each new edition. The value added for this process is that I am curating ideas of others through the search queries I build and the lists I create.

Evernote. While I spend most of my energy collecting content in Evernote, I will share a specific folder or link to a resource.

Pinterest. Pinterest is another place that is getting more attention from me. I will place interesting infographics or articles in Pinterest. All the book reviews I write also make it to Pinterest.

SlideShare. This is the final place I share content. I upload all my presentations to SlideShare. I may also note them in a blog post when I post them.

That is how I try to put in place the Seek-Sense-Share framework. How do you do it?

Invest-Learn-Teach

The idea of Invest-Learn-Teach (ILT) is similar to Seek-Sense-Share in that both stress the importance of sharing what one learns with the rest of the world. For me, this is an essential element. ILT begins with an investment. This investment may take the form of time, money, or resources, but it is an investment in your personal development.[442] As I understand it, a person takes on a personal development quest and invests in books as an example to fulfill this quest. He or she can then conduct in-depth research as part of this investment.

The Learn element of ILT is an application of what one acquired during the investment. True understanding of a topic comes from successfully applying what you learn.[443] Through a continuous reading habit and the application of lessons learned, you can improve your quality of life, business, and overall knowledge. My business has steadily improved because of what I have learned and applied. The investment has been well worth it.

The final element, and the one that resonates the strongest with me, is Teach. The idea of teaching is to share what one has learned for the betterment of the world. Once we have learned something, we have the ability to assist others; this is the time to share or teach. As with Share from Seek-Sense-Share, there are many ways to share what one has learned. Sharing can take the form of blogs, social media, webinars, books, or articles. Through sharing, your credibility and authority on a subject will increase. This in turn will increase your scope of influence. It is a snowballing effect. By sharing, you create new opportunities. These opportunities come about because people will trust you enough to do business with you. This has happened to me. Because of what I have shared, others have asked me to serve on committees, present, and write articles. This is a winning formula for everyone.

Wrap Up

The Seek-Sense-Share and Invest-Learn-Teach frameworks are central to everything I do. They drive my selection of books and other content to read. They help move me from someone who simply acquires knowledge for personal gain to someone who strives to improve the world. Others have followed the same process as they try to make the world a better place. They have selflessly shared what they have learned to help others. If you make learning and sharing central to what you do, you will not only help yourself develop; you will also help others around you grow.

The next section focuses on developing a reading habit

CHAPTER TEN

What to Read

"You must feed your mind with reading material, thoughts, and ideas
that open you to new possibilities." —OPRAH WINFREY

We are now going to put the technical aspects of reading that we
looked at in the last section to practical use. These reading skills will
come in handy as you read different content.

When deciding what to read, you must first know what you want
to achieve. This will help with the reading selection. Narrow the reading selection to the type of material and its modality. Type of material
refers to fiction vs. nonfiction, academic vs. nonacademic, and so on.
Modality refers to printed material, digital, or audio. Each variable can
affect reading goals.

There must be a balance between the reader, the technology, and
the material to become proficient. You must master the technology,
whether it's a printed book, an e-reader, or audio device, to glean the
lessons and wisdom to move forward. You should attain a level of comfort with the technology. There is also a difference between reading
blogs, newspapers, and magazines, and reading books. While one can
certainly learn and benefit from newspapers and magazines, it's important to read books as well.[444] A book reader will gain a longer lasting benefit.

Modality also influences reading. There is a difference in comprehension between reading paper-based books and digital books.[445] One does not read the same on a digital device as a printed book, and note-taking will also be different.[446] It is important to recognize this if you wish to use reading as a way to improve your status in life.

Choose reading material that will help you work better. This cycle of reading and application helps develop experience and wisdom. But do not focus all your reading on business or self-improvement. Take time to read for enjoyment.

Time is valuable, so a reader must understand the reason for reading. Is the reading for entertainment? For inspiration? Is it to learn how to do something? To gain knowledge? Be critical of the quality of the reading material, because it varies. "Some books are carefully researched, well-written, and structured to provide good advice and plausible pathways for learning and change to their readers."[447]

This chapter focuses on reading preferences, finding things to read, and organizing reading. We'll look at reading preferences and modalities first.

Reading Preference

Individuals who read often prefer a modality, or method of reading a book. The modality may change over time or out of necessity, as in the case of General McChrystal, who had to consume more audiobooks due to his demanding work schedule. He "read" while he worked out.

Some read only digital material, some read only printed material, some have taken to audiobooks, and others do not have a preference. My preference is divided between printed books and digital books. I may start with a digital book due to the ease with which I can take notes. But I may get a printed copy of a great book, so I can use it as a desk reference.

Let's look at different reading modalities, starting with printed books.

Books

The latest research indicates there is no real difference in effort between print and digital reading. In some cases, reading on a digital device was easier because of the back lighting. Yet, despite the advancements in e-reading technologies, many people prefer reading printed books for learning.[448] In several studies, people "identified print books as the most 'pleasant' to read."[449] This was in part because the e-readers are not able to duplicate the essential qualities of a physical book. Those qualities include paper pages, a unique weight, a cover, and a binding.

You should determine whether you prefer to read printed or digital text. Which method helps you gather the lessons and wisdom to improve your business, life, and learning? If you struggle to remember what you read when using an e-reader, then you may be more suited for printed books. Learn to recognize your biases early, so you minimize the effort. Figure out what is best for you. With that in mind, let's look at each type.

Print Books

Americans prefer the printed book.[450] There is no fear printed books will disappear completely. With millions upon millions of books in circulation, not all books will become digital.[451] In fact, there has been an increase in print-book publishing and sales in 2015, with a drop-off of digital book sales.[452] It seems millennials are key to this rise in physical book buying.[453] They have an affinity for a bound book. While some bookstores closed during the e-book boom, the number of physical independent stores has begun to recover.[454] This is good news for lovers of print books.

"The book was declared dead with the coming of radio. The hardback was dead with the coming of paperbacks. Print-on-paper was buried fathoms deep by the great god, digital. It was rubbish, all rubbish. Like other aids to reading, such as rotary presses, Linotyping and computer-setting, digital had brought innovation to the dissemination of knowledge and delight. But it was a means, not an end."[455]

There are many benefits of printed books. Here are some to consider:

Printed Books Do Not Run Out of Power. One of the greatest benefits of printed books is they never run out of power like e-readers. You can take a book anywhere and never worry about having to recharge. The only drawback is that when the sun sets, you must find a way to shine a light on the pages.

Printed Books Can Be Cheaper. I buy both newly published books and used books. Great deals can be found, if you're not afraid to buy used books. Many of the books I read are several years old. I can buy these used books at a fraction of the price of a new one.

Printed Books Can Be Easier to Reference. There is a split decision on this item, but it tends to favor printed books. An e-reader will win if you want to search for a specific phrase. But if you need to quickly move from one section of a book to another, a print book is easier. Referencing charts, diagrams, and images is also easier with a printed book.

Printed Books Can Help with Sleep. Physical books may a better choice late in the evening before going to sleep.[456] The light from iPads, phones, computers, and tablets can interfere with one's melatonin production, an important element that helps one sleep. Turn off the electronics and curl up with a book.

Printed Books Support Better Comprehension. How we read affects our comprehension. According to a recent study, readers of printed books can remember events better than those who read the same book on an e-reader.[457] Reading a printed book tends to be a more focused activity than reading on a digital device.[458] Research is showing the actual flipping of pages and other spatial markers helps map content to the brain.[459] These spatial markers include the four corners of a page, the four corners of the book, the number of pages read, and the number of unread pages.[460] An e-reader only sees the four corners of the device. Discerning how much is left to read and how far a reader has already come is very difficult. Creating a mental map is difficult. Because of these issues, some students say they will first print the text if they must learn from a long online section.[461]

Reading speed is another factor that may help comprehension. Reading a traditional printed book can be 20–30 percent faster than reading on a digital device.[462] Reading a printed book helps one stay focused on the content rather than allowing concentration to wander.

However, many research studies indicate individuals who have become comfortable with e-reading achieve the same test scores as those who read printed books.[463] This is good news going forward for those using e-reading devices.

Another observation that has come out of the research is that readers who use a digital device will often not reread a document; nor will they go back to a section for clarification as will readers of paper-based documents.[464]

A reader tends to scan the material on a digital device without engaging in it. Some researchers believe the move to online readers leads to superficial reading and not the deep reading expected in academic work.[465] When reading on screen, readers tend to scan the material and skip a lot of essential content. One factor contributing to the skipping of material is that we now have a lot more material to get through.[466] Readers have adapted reading processes to what is in front of them. Students are recognizing the different levels of concentration on their own. When reading a long text, or when deep reading is necessary, university students prefer to read a printed text.[467]

Physical constraints are a concentration challenge when reading. Eye discomfort increases based on the reading time, the text difficulty, and the medium.[468] "To the extent that the visual discomfort caused by dry eye impacts reading comprehension, printed books will continue to be superior to computer screens, especially when one is trying to read longer, more challenging texts,"[469] although the discomfort gap is closing with improvements to screen technology.

Distractions also have an impact on concentration. Printed books have few distractions and yield a higher level of comprehension.[470] Digital documents often have hyperlinks to more resources. This results in a higher cognitive load because the reader must make decisions. The distraction may be the presence of a link. This affects reading speed, concentration, and comprehension.

E-books

E-reading devices are finding their way into the homes of readers. According to the Pew Research Center, 50 percent of Americans now own an e-reading device such as a tablet computer or an e-reader.[471] This has led to increased levels of reading. "Adults who own e-readers like Kindles or Nooks read e-books more frequently than those who only own other devices (like tablets or cell phones)."[472] American adults are reading books on smartphones because of the convenience.

Many adults will consume a book in different modalities. They may start reading on their e-reader and then read a chapter or two on their smartphones. They may first read a book on a digital device and then buy a printed copy as a ready reference.

E-Reading Continues to Rise

The number of people who read an e-book during the past year rose from 11 percent in 2011 to 28 percent in 2014.[473] In 2012, at least 43 percent of Americans sixteen years and older had read an e-book.[474] Between 2008 and 2010, e-book sales skyrocketed and resulted in many physical bookstores closing.[475] Since then, the excitement for digital content has waned to a steady point of about 20 percent of the market. While some prefer print or digital, others prefer to read what is available, regardless of the modality.

Academic Use of E-books

In the academic environment, 40 percent of students and faculty prefer to use e-books.[476] This preference will continue to rise as more curriculum and supporting text goes online. More and more academic departments are adopting digital resources and open-educational resources. Adopting content that uses the best features interactive e-books allow is important to them.

E-readers Read More

Those who read e-books or use e-readers tend to read more than those who only read printed books.[477] "The average tablet owner reads 24 books per year, compared to other readers, who read an average of 15 books per year."[478] Digital readers read more books in varying formats. The type of device did not seem to matter. Additionally, individuals who own an e-reading device for longer than one year read more compared to those who are new e-reader owners.

Lighten the Load with Digital Books

One of the greatest benefits of digital books is that a reader can carry hundreds of books without added weight. I packed thousands of books when I recently moved across the country. Moving these books took a physical toll.

E-book Preference

People prefer one format over another depending upon the situation.[479] People who are traveling and need quick access to a book, or those looking for variety, tend to prefer a digital format. They tend to favor a printed book if they want to read to children or share a book with others.

Easier to Add Notes to Digital Note-Taking Devices

I prefer using digital books when I want to highlight on the device and move them to Zotero or other digital note-taking applications. The highlighted text in a Kindle can be copied and pasted into a digital note-taking application.

However, as previously stated, finding key information is a challenge in a digital book. Navigating on an e-reader to a specific place in a book can be more challenging than in a printed book.[480] E-books are also not consistent in their design and operation. Some e-books have a table of contents and others do not. Some digital books offer search capabilities; others do not. Some e-books use page numbers and others do not. This becomes a challenge when trying to cite a passage found in a digital document. Readers also complain of disorientation while searching through a digital book.[481]

Difficulty Taking Notes

Note-taking is another challenge with e-book software.[482] While I have had success taking notes and highlighting content on my Kindle, not all e-reading programs are the same. Even with the Kindle, not all documents work the same. For example, I often have difficulty taking notes and exporting notes from a PDF file.

Difficult Referencing Content

One of the greatest challenges with e-books is referencing them like a printed book.[483] Jumping from section to section is very easy. More effort is needed with an e-book to reference other parts of the book. E-books are easier to read in a linear manner.

E-books can be more powerful learning tools than printed books when digital features such as glossaries, videos, audio, and embedded questions enhance the text.[484] However, some studies indicate that these digital features could be distractions.[485]

Increasing E-reading Comfort

Readers are not yet as comfortable with e-readers as they are with printed books, but their comfort levels are rising.[486] Increasing the size of the text is one of the greatest benefits of reading an e-book.[487] A reader is more reliant on glasses or other magnifying devices reading a paper-based book.

More people will use e-readers as primary reading devices as the technology improves. Speed to adoption will increase by teaching learners how to use e-reading devices for reading and learning while in school. As I noted, more and more schools are moving to digital content.

E-book File Format

There are no definitive standards for e-book file types. Each e-book company developing e-readers has a book format unique to their device.[488] Readers who buy an Amazon Kindle or a Barnes and Noble Nook are generally restricted to purchasing digital books from that company. The good news is that most e-reading devices also can import PDF files and some generic e-book file types.

More Distractions

Those who are reading with electronic devices are more susceptible to distraction.[489] Links and social media applications can take them away from reading. Because many e-book readers are reading books on their phones or iPads, other programs with notifications can call them away. Additionally, reading in outdoor light is challenging on some e-readers.

Audiobooks

Audiobooks are another popular way to consume books. In 2014, 14 percent of adults reported listening to an audiobook.[490] Those who are more affluent (63 percent) listen to audiobooks more than the poor (5 percent).[491] Often, readers listen to audiobooks during commutes to and from work.

Listening to Audiobooks While Doing Other Tasks

I often listen to a podcast while I drive or walk. I do not listen to audiobooks because I tend to read nonfiction and like to take a lot of notes. However, I can see myself listening to fiction as I drive or walk.

Audiobooks are great ways to consume books while performing other tasks. "Readers" can listen to a book while commuting, walking, or involved in other endeavors. They can listen to a book while working out. I know one individual who listens to audiobooks while swimming. That is certainly not possible with a printed or digital book.

Listening as Good as Reading

According to research highlighted on the Curiosity.com website, readers benefit as much from listening to a book as reading it. The brain works on the language aspect with the same amount of effort, even though it's using two different processes.

Reading Magazines and Trade Journals

While reading books is the focus of this book, you can derive great benefit from reading magazines and trade journals in your field. You can develop a competitive advantage by seeking out new ideas in these resources.[492] When I was working as a webmaster for two different colleges, I would look forward to the newest issue of monthly technology magazines. These magazines would help me put in place a new feature or make a tweak in our systems. In most cases, the articles were well beyond my experience level. Yet, when I reviewed past issues, I would often surprise myself by finding a needed solution. My experience had caught up to what I had read.

Finding Content to Read

Always have a stack of books ready to read, because professional reading is so important to investing in personal learning. There are many ways to find books that can help you develop.

- Book lists
- Book reviews
- References in books
- Follow specific writers
- Problem-solving capabilities
- Recommendations from friends and mentors
- Book recommendation sites
- Digital bookstores
- Physical bookstores
- Used books
- Conferences
- Podcasts, blogs, and YouTube videos
- Book clubs
- Libraries

Book Lists

As noted earlier, book lists are an important learning tool for organizations. They are a way for leaders to help set the vision and culture of an organization. They are not only useful for organizations; book lists can help you find books to fuel personal learning.

You can find book lists in many places, such as

- Amazon Best Seller lists (http://www.amazon.com/gp/bestsellers/)
- *New York Times* Best Seller List (http://www.nytimes.com/books/best-sellers/?_r=0)
- *USA Today*'s Best-Selling Books list (http://www.usatoday.com/life/books/best-selling/)
- *Publisher's Weekly* Best Sellers List (http://www.publishersweekly.com/pw/nielsen/)
- NPR Bestseller Lists (http://www.npr.org/books/bestsellers/)

Many of these put books into categories such as fiction, nonfiction, and religion. Keeping an eye on these lists will help you find something useful to read.

Also, there are lists compiled by entrepreneurs, business leaders, and political leaders. Many of these successful people are happy to share the books that led to their success. Warren Buffett, for example, shares books with new and old acquaintances, and also recommends books to read in his annual letters to Berkshire Hathaway shareholders.[493]

However, you should always feel free to branch out. Novelist Haruki Murakami offers the cautionary thought that someone who reads what everyone else is reading will think what everyone else is thinking.[494]

Book Reviews

Book reviews are another way to find new books to read, as well as new perspectives about a book you may have read.[495] Readers can find book reviews in the *London Review of Books* and the *New York Review of Books*. There are book reviews in many academic journals. Books listed on Amazon, for example, often have reviews by readers and publications that one can peruse. I look at the variety and quantity of reviews before I buy. I will often get the book if there are numerous good reviews.

References in Books

Another place to find recommendations for books to read is in the books one is already reading. Very often, authors will recommend other books to read or have a reference list they used while writing the book. The reference list or bibliography is usually at the end of the book.

Follow Specific Writers

One of the factors to consider is the author. Is the author someone who is well known? Have you read other books from the same author and do you respect what the author has written? If I like a specific author, I will often seek out the author's other books. Writers are a "known brand." Relying upon a known brand or writer can provide a sense of security.

Choose Books to Solve Problems

To find a book to read, you may not have to look further than the problem you are trying to solve. If you are having marketing issues, you should seek out a good marketing book. If you are trying to launch a startup, look for books to help craft a strategy.

Recommendations from Friends or Mentors

Personal learning networks are great places to get recommendations for new books and articles to read. Quite often, members of a network offer suggestions based on their experiences. In many cases, family, friends, and coworkers offer recommendations for books to read. These individuals will try to be helpful and recommend books they believe are beneficial, and they will discourage you from reading books that are not appropriate for your needs. The recommendation is strongest when the individual making the recommendation has read the book. It should be from someone whose opinion you respect.

Readers can also ask their network for suggestions. If they would rather not bother their network, they could follow influencers and see what they mention. I learn about many of the books I read from the podcasts I listen to.

Book Recommendation Sites

Book recommendation sites are another place to get reading suggestions. These allow you to see what is popular; search based on subject, title, or author; and peruse reader comments. Recommendation algorithms such as those on Amazon are becoming more and more helpful in finding books one may like.[496] Here are some of the more popular book recommendation sites:

- Amazon—http://www.amazon.com/
- Goodreads—http://www.goodreads.com/

- Gnooks—http://gnooks.com/
- Library Thing—http://www.librarything.com/
- What Should I Read Next? —http://whatshouldireadnext.com/

Digital Bookstores

I am addicted to digital bookstores. In digital bookstores like Amazon and Barnes and Noble, customers can search the entire inventory in seconds. If I am faced with a new problem or come across a new area I want to learn more about, I will conduct a search for books on the topic. Using a Kindle device, I can have the book in my hands in seconds. I am not alone—"75 percent of e-book readers start their search at an online bookstore or website."[497] Digital bookstores are the second-most popular place for new book recommendations. Those living in an urban community will take advantage of digital bookstore opportunities more than those living in suburban and rural communities.[498]

Physical Bookstores

The staff at physical bookstores can make great recommendations. According to a Pew Research Center survey, 31 percent of e-reader owners get their recommendations from physical bookstores.[499] While many expected the number of physical bookstores to decline due to surge of digital books and online booksellers, there has been a 27 percent increase in independent bookstores in the United States since 2009.[500] These are still great places to go to find something to read. Used bookstores are also great places to find a book, especially at a discount.

Used Books

There are many ways to pick up some great books to read at a great price if you like the thrill of the hunt. Readers can find wonderful used books at used bookstores, thrift stores, garage sales, flea markets, yard sales, antique malls, Craigslist, eBay, estate sales, and library sales. You will be giving up time for money in most deals by venturing into physical stores. I have built a sizable collection by buying used books.

Conferences

I stock up on reading at professional conferences. My two conferences of choice are the Association of Talent Development and Social Media Marketing World. These conferences have extensive bookstores. Additionally, a significant number of vendors also sell books. I enjoy picking up books at these conferences because I have an opportunity to meet the authors and listen to them speak. Many conferences provide packing and shipping services to help send books home.

Podcasts, Blogs, and YouTube Videos

Listening to authors talk about their book or program is another great way to find a new book. I have added hundreds of recommended books to my reading list by listening to podcasts or reading blog articles. Often, the podcast guests have written their own books. If the guest is especially interesting, I will attempt to learn more by reading the guest author's book.

Book Clubs

Book clubs are another place to learn about new books. Readers can often find a local book club through their library, or can create their own clubs. Book clubs can be face-to-face meetings or online, and provide an opportunity to network and learn from others. They challenge readers to commit to completing books they agree to read, and encourage readers to read books they would not select on their own. Because there is a deadline, there is more pressure to complete the reading. Some communities have adopted a "one city, one book" model, in which the community encourages the entire population of the city to read a book together. They then sponsor activities to discuss the book.[501]

The social aspect of a book club will also help readers remember more of the book. For example, readers can increase the social component of a book club by discussing a book over a meal; this is a tactic Oprah Winfrey uses.[502]

Book Club Recommendations

Here are some suggestions for making selections for a book club:[503]

- Try to select books that will resonate with members. If it's a work-related club, find books to help move the industry forward.
- Do not overwhelm members with a long, complicated book. Time is a consideration.
- Vary the book selection to appeal to the tastes of all members.
- Continue to look for books through other professional sources, such as magazines, forums, and newsletters.
- Consider recommendations from club members.

Libraries

"Libraries are the thin red line between civilization and barbarism."
—Neil Gaiman

Public libraries hold a special place when it comes to the power of reading. Ever since Ben Franklin developed the concept of a public library, the public library has been one of the cornerstones of a community. A library is a place where people can go to learn. It doesn't matter one's status in life; readers are always welcome.

Libraries Are Cornerstones of a Community

The library is one of the cornerstones of a community or college. Urban, suburban, and rural segments of our society believe a library is important.[504] Many Americans feel a loss of a "local library would be a blow to the community."[505]

Librarians are a valuable research tool. They can help you find a book. Moderate readers (six to twenty books per year) from rural areas will often get book recommendations from local libraries.[506] If the library does not have the book or article in stock, there are agreements with other libraries to have it loaned to a borrower.

Who Uses the Library?

Younger Americans (ages sixteen and seventeen) are more likely to visit a library compared to those sixty-five and older.[507] This may be primarily due to their attendance at school or an encouraging parent. Fifty-nine percent of the younger crowd visited the library in 2013, whereas only 39 percent of those sixty-five and older did. Urban and suburban audiences are the highest owners of library cards, in large part due to their proximity to community libraries.[508] However, these segments used the library differently. Those living in the suburbs are most likely to have checked out a printed book or audiobook during the past year. "As a rule, people who have extensive economic, social, technological, and cultural resources are also more likely to use and value libraries as part of those networks."[509] Those with higher education and income use the library more.[510] Perhaps people with these characteristics have realized the importance of active reading.

People tend to use a library when they are working through a unique problem or life stage. If the period of time is unfamiliar, a reader will use references to become more familiar with the situation. Expectant couples will often do a lot of reading prior to a birth of a child—especially a first child.

Libraries Are Digitizing

Those directing libraries have always been forward-thinking. They recognize they must consider current technologies and adapt for the future. Thus, libraries are also moving to digital and audio collections. Book publishers have been the slowing point in this migration. The publishers have been charging a higher rate to libraries for access to electronic editions, but publishers are now beginning to realize that providing electronic copies may be beneficial.[511]

Borrowing e-books from the library has not yet taken hold.[512] In 2012, only 13 percent reported borrowing an e-book from a library. This will change due to the increase of e-reading devices in the hands of the public as well as an increase in awareness that the library can lend e-books.[513]

When asked if they would be willing to check out an e-reader preloaded with e-books, urban and suburban groups were most likely to pursue the offer.[514] The staff at your local library would be happy to help you learn how to use e-books and audiobooks if you are unfamiliar with the technology. This could expand options for getting more reading done.

A digital copy of a book can be checked out for a period of time, just like physical books. Readers must have an application loaded on their computer or mobile device and have an account with their library. Here are applications libraries may be using:

- Overdrive
- SimplyE

Why Some Do Not Use Libraries

Shane Parrish says: "If you're not keeping what you read, you probably want to think about what you're reading and how."[515] I agree; it is not possible to take notes in library books as you would in your own book. This should not keep you out of a library, though. "Those who use libraries are more likely than others to be book buyers and actually prefer to buy books rather than borrow them."[516] It is not only library patrons who like to buy books; most print book and e-book readers buy their own books.[517] Additionally, over half of audiobook listeners prefer to borrow their audiobooks.[518]

Libraries Yield a Cost Savings

A librarian at the University of Wyoming reported she had checked out twenty-four e-books from the public library, for a savings of approximately $250 had she purchased the same books from Amazon.[519] She added that she did not calculate the savings of academic books and journal articles checked out of the library.

If you don't have money to buy books, consider visiting your local library, where you can read for free.

Build Your Own Library

Some people are content with using their public library as their personal library, yet many of us have built our own libraries. In order to appreciate and understand some influential books, you may have to reread them. While there are only a couple of books I have reread in their entirety, I have a ready reference section on my shelf of books I frequent.

One recommendation to consider is putting together a special collection of 150 books with which you develop a special bond.[520] "This way you develop a relationship with the teachings and the author and return to the book when you have questions. The teachings become imprinted in your mind, are stored in long term memory and become part of your belief system."[521]

Read on a Variety of Subjects

Regardless of where one finds reading material, there are important overlying considerations when making the actual selections. Although I have touched on these issues throughout the book, it bears repeating. Read within your field of interest if you're reading for professional development. But also read more widely, including books on history, literature, and philosophy. Pursue a liberal arts perspective on reading. This helps develop a creative-thinking mindset. Make the necessary pivots in reading content as you advance in your career. For example, if an individual becomes a manager or leader, he or she should start reading more books in those areas.

Primary source documents, old books, and books in different fields of study are also a great way to understand the development of an idea or concept.[522] Rather than rely on an interpretation of what someone said, you can read the original document. Source documents do not have to be ancient manuscripts. Each day, people write hundreds of original documents.

Likewise, there are amazing things to learn while reading old books. I recently read *Think and Grow Rich* by Napoleon Hill. He wrote it in 1937, but it remains one of the most-read books. I have a couple of other books written during this period on my list, one from Dale Carnegie and another by Hill. Many of the solutions proposed decades and even centuries ago are applicable today.

One of the best ways to discover new ideas is to combine two different concepts. To discover new concepts, read popular books in different fields. While reading, you may find a gap in an area on which you can capitalize. Take a chance, and read something new, outside of your comfort zone.

Organizing Reading

There are many applications available to help manage a library. In addition to Goodreads, the *Inside Higher Ed* article "7 Apps for Cataloguing Your Home Library" shares several applications.[523]

- Libib
- iBookshelf
- Libri
- My Library

- Book Crawler
- Home Library
- iCollect Books Pro

I have not used these specific applications, so I cannot speak for them. However, here are some features a reader might want to keep in mind when looking for an application:

- Scan in books with a barcode.
- Categorize books with tags.
- Search.
- Ability to write reviews or give starred reviews.
- Track location of a book.
- Track book lending.
- Export a library.
- Wish lists.

Wrap Up

This chapter focused on the "what" of reading. Readers can read printed material such as books and magazines. They can consume reading material in a digital format using an e-reader. They can also listen to audiobooks, which is great if commuting.

There are an incredible number of ways to find great content to read. Search references and reviews online, or from friends, librarians, or bookstore staff.

There are several options available for collecting and organizing reading. Digital applications can help you track your reading.

Go out and find something good to read!

Next, we will get others involved in reading. Specifically, we will look at reading and the organization. Some of the strategies include ways for encouraging reading, developing book lists, and building organizational libraries.

CHAPTER ELEVEN

Reading and the Organization

By now, you've probably realized that I do not think reading is a solo act. Reading is a conversation with the author and with others with whom one shares discoveries. There is no better place to share what one learns than the workplace. Whether you work on an assembly line or in an executive suite, you should read to improve the organization and share what you have learned.

This chapter examines the impact of learning on an organization, how reading should be encouraged and supported in an organization, and how leaders play an essential role.

Learning and the Organization

Leaders in successful organizations realize success is dependent upon the skills and knowledge of their employees. Employees must stay current on ever-changing information for an organization to become or remain successful.[524] The leaders who do not learn this lesson see their organizations become irrelevant and obsolete.[525] Organizations would have an easier time being successful if they could teach their employees what they need to know just once, but single-training approaches are often inadequate. Most employees realize the importance of remaining current and trying to resolve problems in a shifting environment.[526] Information changes, thus creating new problems employees must solve. Organization leadership and training sections must foster an atmosphere that encourages learning.

Changing Information

Things move faster today than they did a century ago. This affects the workplace and the need to stay abreast of constant changes. Information or knowledge in different fields becomes obsolete in a matter of years rather than lifetimes.[527] The lifespan of knowledge varies according to the discipline. As a result, employees need to continue to learn to stay current or to get ahead in the workplace.[528] Not long ago, corporate trainers could prepare individuals for lifelong employment with a single training program.[529] This is no longer possible. Today, even periodic courses do not help employees stay current in a changing world.[530] Employees need to augment any organizational training they receive with informal learning. An employee's access to books is one of the most powerful tools to help their informal learning—employees should recognize that they need to be lifelong learners.

Impact Employees Have on Organization

Organizational learning is about developing the employee. The onus is not only on the organization and its leadership; employees also have a responsibility to improve the organization.[531] Organizations have been reducing the amount of training they provide, and many companies now require employees to manage their own learning.[532] Employees need to stay current through informal learning or risk replacement.[533]

Employees tend to apply the information they acquire in an informal learning environment to real problems they are solving.[534] People learn because of the challenges they must overcome.[535] Employees learn to solve problems through on-the-job training, from mentors, and through self-exploration. Reading is a key method for self-exploration.[536]

Certain learning approaches may be more effective than others. Employers should allow employees to determine the method, schedule, resources, and reason for training.[537] However, organizations need to develop methods to help employees stay current. These methods may require employees to seek more education or participate in organizational training. Time is an important issue; employees cannot expect to learn on their off time.[538] Employers must make time available during work hours. They also need to arrange work areas for quiet study time. Experienced employees should be active contributors to workplace learning opportunities.

Impact of Organizational Leaders

Whether an organization supports learning is in large part due to leadership. Leaders who recognize the importance of a learning culture empower employees and provide them with tools and learning opportunities.[539] Top management must have a commitment to the process and concept, and must remove policies that impede learning.[540] Managers and supervisors should be proactive in helping employees identify learning needs, goals, and resources. Employers must ensure employees are working to meet organization goals by identifying knowledge gaps. Managers should know what employees need to do and their weak areas. Managers also need to help employees understand their roles in the organization and how they can advance; employers can do this by ensuring employees are applying what they are learning.[541] They must also determine how to measure success.

Managers will take on more responsibilities of developing and maintaining a learning environment, if the organization develops into a learning-centric organization. Managers must take on a more mentoring role in an informal learning environment.[542] Further, managers must develop into good learning coaches and must devote more time to that purpose.[543] They need to receive training to assume their new roles as coach and learning mentor. They must also become better subject-matter experts.

The role of a manager or supervisor has changed from one of controlling behavior to one of employee development.[544] The supervisor is key to developing the right attitude about informal learning; he or she should lead by example. Methods for leading by example are: pay for training, reward learning champions, make learning a job requirement, and recognize learning achievements. Organizational leaders from every level should lead organization training and learning, stress its importance to the organization, and show personal learning. Organizational leaders should share the books and articles they are reading and create opportunities for employees to mingle and exchange ideas.[545]

Reading in the Organization

Reading does not have to be a solo activity. Active reading across an organization can help the organization become better. However, leaders can do more at the organizational level to encourage reading.

Employers can apply many of the lessons learned while studying the reading habits of college students. Like students, employees are more inclined to read if leaders encourage them and provide choices.

Business leaders can support professional reading by providing professional reading libraries and reading lists.

Encourage Professional Reading

Organizations can support informal learning by encouraging professional reading as well as sharing current articles, magazines, and books being read as part of staff discussions.[546] However, while managers should encourage their employees to read, they should not require them to read.[547] Nothing kills motivation more than to require something. Instead, they should attempt to weave discussion about what they are reading into regular conversation. If you read a book or an article, share it with others in the workplace; they might enjoy it.[548] On a regular basis, I recommend books and articles that others will find useful. During my weekly team meeting, I ask my team members what they are reading as well as share my recently read books. Don't simply ask team members what they are reading; help them develop comprehension and critical thinking. Try to tie the reading to what they are doing on the job and how it applies. What is the impact of what they are reading?

Reading can be a cost-effective means for advancing professional development.[549] Researchers have found that public school teachers are not reading at a professional level.[550] They cited barriers to professional reading, including:

- Lack of time
- Overwhelmed by the amount of material
- Held back by the technical language

Strategies for promoting increased reading for professional development include:[551]

- Encourage reading at all levels of the organization, especially from the leadership.
- Leadership needs to model appropriate reading behavior.
- Highlighting specific journals, books, or articles to be read.
- Providing time to read at work.
- Promote reading at meetings and in-service training opportunities.
- Place appropriate reading material in break areas.
- Develop professional reading libraries.
- Reference appropriate books and articles while discussing solutions to problems.
- Invest in journals dedicated to specialized fields rather than generalist content.

Reading Lists

What we learn shapes what we do and how we do it. You can learn a lot about leadership and business by reading the books recommended by those who have gone before. Organizational leaders should share the books and articles they are reading.[552] Many leaders do this through reading lists. Reading lists can help ground a company in the vision leaders have for the organization. When I was in the Air Force, the Air Force chief of staff encouraged us to read the books on his reading list. According to General Fogleman, the originator of the list, "The objective was to broaden understanding of air and space power and to examine how they should be employed in independent, joint, and coalition operations."[553] The original list emphasized different levels of an airman's professional development. "It includes a basic list for captains, an intermediate list for majors and lieutenant colonels, and an advanced list for colonels and general officers."[554] Each year, the Air Force chief of staff updated and shared the professional reading list.

You can get an idea of what the Air Force chief of staff wanted to emphasize through the 2016 list (http://static.dma.mil/usaf/csafreadinglist2017/). The chiefs of staff for other branches of the military also created reading lists with a particular topic being emphasized. "There is simply no better way to prepare for the future than a disciplined, focused commitment to a personal course of reading, study, thought, and reflection."[555]

The military is not the only organization that has reading lists.

Jeff Bezos, CEO of Amazon, has a reading list for his organization. The list is to help develop a common framework for employees and executives in his organization.[556] Bill Gates maintains his recommended reading list on his site called Gatesnotes. For the past seventeen years, J. P. Morgan has published a recommended reading list on its website. The list has ten books on a diverse array of topics.

Many academic institutions also publish reading lists. For example, the University of California, Berkeley, has offered a reading list for its incoming freshmen and transfer students each year since 1985. Other schools, such as Yale University, develop reading lists for specific topics like "Managing at Yale Recommended Reading List." I remember receiving a recommended reading list for adult education and instructional technology put together at the University of Wyoming.

Reading lists alone are not enough. Reading must be stressed constantly if a manager wants employees to increase reading.[557] There must be regular conversation about reading and books that can improve the organization.

Establish a Library

Establishing workplace libraries is a great way to encourage employees to support their self-directed learning through professional reading.[558] This library can also be virtual.[559] Establishing a library and referencing the library in a workplace stresses the importance of continuous learning. Lt. General Van Riper purchased six thousand books for the unit libraries under his command.[560] The Marine Corps Association and Foundation has been assisting Marine Corps units in developing a library.[561] They are focusing on building libraries for deploying organizations and Marine units in remote locations. The books chosen come from the Commandant of the Marine Corps professional reading list. The Marine Corps requires marines to read some of the books listed on the reading list each year. Having a location where they can check them out helped increase success with the reading program. Additionally, the librarians load 350 books on Kindle devices that Marines can check out of the library. This is an idea other organizations can adopt to help promote their reading programs.

The first thing I did when I took my new job was bring my professional library to work to share with my team. It now has a prominent place in our new office space. We have extended this professional library to include a virtual library of e-books. We store our e-books in Google Drive for the team to share. This was to encourage a reading program at every level of my department.

Wrap Up

Everyone in the organization needs to dedicate time to learning, in order to keep the organization improving and current. Professional reading is an excellent way to shape a company culture as well as spread common knowledge through the organization. The military has come to understand the value of reading for the entire organization. They developed reading lists to promote reading at all levels. Other companies have followed suit. An ever-growing library is one of the most cost-effective ways to promote lifelong learning. Selecting the right books can have a lasting effect on an organization.

The next chapter focuses on developing a personal library. However, the lessons can be also applied to building an organizational library.

CHAPTER TWELVE

Build a Personal Library

Personal libraries have been a centerpiece of knowledge and learning for our titans of government, military, and industry. Jefferson, Roosevelt, Patton, and Gates have cherished their libraries. Patton and McChrystal fought wars and regularly referenced their libraries. Jefferson and Adams helped build a nation with their libraries at ready reference. Gates and Jobs used their libraries to build their industries.

Personal libraries provide a ready source of information to help solve problems or provide inspiration. In this chapter, we will look at how personal libraries can help promote lifelong learning, spark new ideas, and generate memories. We will also learn how to develop and manage a personal library.

Libraries Can Promote Lifelong Learning

Promoting lifelong learning in a household, company, or volunteer organization begins with a library. Many successful leaders who understand the role of reading in their achievements and their ability to remain current have developed personal libraries as part of their commitment to lifelong learning. Also, according to research, there is a strong connection between having books available that are being read and academic achievement.[562]

Books Are Available for Future Reference

The ability to reference books one has read is one of the obvious reasons for building a personal library.[563] I cannot count the number of times I have referenced my library to pull together a collection of books to help solve a problem. Certainly, one can create a library for many purposes, but my focus is on reference libraries. While I have many novels in my library, it is primarily a reference facility.

A Reminder of What One Has Learned

Books can serve as physical reminders of what is learned.[564] A reader can recall what a book is about by glancing at a cover or perusing a few pages. If a book is in your library, you can keep going back to reread key passages. "A book that is reread is the highest praise for an author."[565]

You approach a book from a more enlightened perspective when rereading. If you keep notes in your books, you will be able to see what was important to you at a specific period. You can add to your thinking as you reread the book. These layers of notes will help show your growth over the years.

Libraries Tell Your Story

Presidential libraries are special places because they tell a story about the person who owned the books. What makes up the collection helps tell what was important to the owner. If you were to look at my library, you would find books about computer programming, instructional design, leadership, productivity, martial arts, magic, history, military history, and much more. You would see my changing interests if you took snapshots of my book collection at various periods of my life. Some interests faded away while others became more prominent. My books would also let you know that I place great importance on learning. This collection of books helps to tell my story. In my house, a visitor will also see what topics are important to my wife and what topics are important to us as a couple.

Your Library Speaks Volumes About Other People

"Having a personal library in your house functions as a good litmus test for people who come over. If their first question is 'WOW, have you read all these?' it says something about them. If they immediately start looking for books they like or start inspecting the titles like it's a bookstore, that says something, too. You can tell a lot about a person based on their relationship to reading."[566]

How to Build and Maintain a Library

A personal library is a lifelong investment in time and money. Build it with care. Physical books provide attributes not available with e-books and audiobooks. A printed book library can be scanned for a needed title. Electronic and audiobooks tend to stay out of sight and thus out of mind. I have hundreds of electronic books at my disposal, but I do not reference them as often or in the same way as printed books.

I will focus on physical libraries when discussing the building of a personal library. Here are suggestions for building a library that will be the envy of the neighborhood—or at least bring order to one's life.

Finding the Right Space for a Library

There are many things to consider when creating a library. First, think about location. This means thinking about lighting, ventilation, comfort, and shelving.

Library Location

I have always dreamt of having a house where I could build a dedicated library for the whole collection. However, I am usually settling for makeshift library spaces. I have two large bookcases in my office and a loft in my house with a large collection of books. Additionally, we have many smaller bookcases spread throughout the house.

Consider the available space when planning a library. You may have to negotiate if you share your living space with others. Are there rooms that can be dedicated as a library? Think about the type and amount of lighting. Excess lighting can damage books. If planning to put a library in a basement, will it be susceptible to flooding? Are there insect and rodent issues? Some of these critters love to eat books. Is the area humid? Mold and mildew have ruined many books. I learned some of these lessons the hard way!

Also consider the decor when putting together a library. At a minimum, you should have a reading chair, table, rug, and light.[567] Other decorations like artwork can help make it a pleasant retreat.

Bookshelves

Proper bookshelves are essential to any library. Decide whether to build bookshelves, buy them, or use alternative bookshelves. If you intend to build your own shelves, there are some very good books on the market to help guide you. If you have some woodworking talent,

194

IKEA Billy Bookcases can be converted into built-in shelves. I am a fan of Billy Bookcases. They are easily assembled and can be arranged in many clever configurations. Another option is buy and repurpose used bookcases with paint or stain.[568] Leah French from *The Spruce* also recommends using alternative materials for bookshelves such as crates, ladders and boards, cinder blocks and boards, and so on. Other ideas for alternative bookshelves include using thin utility storage shelves.

Ensure the bookshelves can hold the weight of the books and can be adjusted to accommodate different-sized books. You will also need to plan for a ladder if building floor-to-ceiling bookcases. A library ladder rolls along a rail.

Filling the Library

Put together a plan.[569] A librarian has a plan; a hoarder does not. When you select a book for your collection, you should have specific intent. A new addition to your library should fit in a specific collection. If you do not have a collection for the book, you then must decide if you need to create a new collection or not. This will help create a library that is special.

Buy Books

A reader must invest in books to build a personal library. Remember, this is an investment in lifelong learning. Over time, you'll see your interests develop and change. Not only will you add to the library through buying books; you will also add to the library with your own thoughts. Because you bought the book, you own it. You can take notes in the book and have a dialogue with the author—things you would be unable to do with a library book.

If you want to keep costs down, buy used books. This is something I do, especially for foundational books. I can often find them listed on Amazon for one cent. I do not care if someone has read them before. Likewise, I do not care if they are soft or hardcover. I have also benefited from the marginalia others have left in used books. The investment in books can be used as a tax deduction depending upon the business.

Avoid Kindle and Audiobooks

Kindle and audiobooks are not appropriate when developing a personal library.[570] While there are benefits for purchasing a Kindle or audiobook, they do not lend themselves to finding information quickly. You must first remember which book the information is in or review your notes to recall the contents of interest. However, simply looking at the cover of a physical book will quite often trigger a memory. I still have a healthy Kindle habit. However, if I find a book I like, I will often buy a physical copy.

Organizing the Library

A library needs some type of organization. This doesn't mean you must install a card catalog or use the Dewey Decimal System. But placing similar books together will make finding a book easier when needed. All my adult education books are together, as are my military history books. As noted before, I have extra categories. For example, I have one section dedicated to my reading list. When I buy new books, I add them to this shelf. I then always have something lined up to read. When I finish reading a book, I place it in one of the other categories.

Many people arrange books by color or size. One convenient arrangement of books is by tallest to smallest in each category. Other suggestions for organizing categories include alphabetical, chronological, and read and unread.[571] Alphabetizing books works better for fiction than nonfiction. Arranging books in chronological order can be a good way to show one's life path.

Inventorying Books

There are many options for maintaining an inventory of books. Keep a list in a notebook or on a spreadsheet. Go old school and build a card catalog. You can also find card catalog cabinets on eBay, flea markets, or antique malls. You'll then need to fill out the cards.

Consider an electronic card catalog like a public library if you want to take your library to the next level. One of the benefits of having an electronic inventory is that the inventory remains safe from physical harm in the event of disaster. A collection can be accessed from a mobile phone with a library application. This is very useful when exploring bookstores.

Listing a book on more than one shelf is another benefit of having a digital listing of books.[572] However, I recommend having a way to find the book on its physical shelf. The virtual shelves could be useful for browsing through an application.

There are many library-application options. Here are some things to consider:

- Online or desktop
- Mobile application compatible
- Free or paid
- Enter books manually, by ISBN, or by scanning
- Search based on title, author, publisher, year, or ISBN

- Quantity of books one can add
- Borrowing or loaning ability
- Ability to export database
- Integration with other applications, such as Goodreads
- Categories such as genres and location

List of Applications

Here are some applications to explore for managing a library:

- LibraryThing
- Reader2
- Delicious Monster
- BookCAT
- Collectorz.com Book Collector
- Readerware
- Libib
- iBookshelf
- Libri
- My Library
- Book Crawler
- Home Library
- iCollect Books Pro

Prune the Library

Libraries need to be pruned every once in a while. Occasionally, take an honest look at your library and remove the books you no longer need. These can be given to charity organizations or sold.

Creating Special Collections

A special collection could be created when building the library. For example, in my library, I have built a collection of Civil Air Patrol aerospace education books from the 1940s to the present. The collection shows the changes in aviation and spaceflight. When the program started, there were no jet engines. Any particular topic of interest, such as a collection of books about weird animals, has a place in a personal library.[573] Another section could be finding books one read and loved as a child.

Wrap Up

Personal libraries can be a powerful addition to one's home, office, or work. They provide ready references in times of need. A well-developed library is not something to do haphazardly. Take time to select the right books, create the appropriate furnishings, and build useful shelves. Organize the books on the shelves so you have easy access to them. There are a number of ways to organize the books and record what is in the collection.

Now that you have set up a library, it is time to do something with it. This is the time for you to put sharing what you have learned into practice. The last chapter encourages you to share and teach what you gain from reading.

CHAPTER THIRTEEN

Doing Something with What You Read

"If you don't have time to read, you don't have the time (or the tools) to write. Simple as that." —Stephen King

We are coming to the end of our journey. As you have discovered, reading is an effective way to gain knowledge about a subject. But reading becomes even more powerful when you put into practice what you've learned. Sharing and teaching are the third parts of the Seek-Sense-Share and Invest-Learn-Teach frameworks. Sharing is more than giving something away. For instance, you can share by improving your business processes—others using those processes will also benefit. You can also share by teaching others.

This chapter focuses on putting to use what you have learned. This can be improving your practice, sharing what you have learned, and sharing what you have read.

Improve Practices

Strengthening knowledge is critical to lifelong development. Reading is a great way to build upon knowledge. But reading is only part of development. To fully develop, you must do something with what you have read. You must synthesize and evaluate what you read. If you're an entrepreneur, for example, you can reflect upon what is read and determine if it will help advance your business. The lessons learned can be incorporated into your processes and procedures.

When I read, I am reflecting on how I can use what I am reading to improve my operations. My team and I tweak what we are doing. My colleagues are often quite amused when I walk into work on Monday morning with my notebook of new ideas. We discuss them as a team and decide what changes we need to make. I will then change processes to reflect our decisions.

Sharing What You've Learned

Take time to share what you learn through presentations, blogs, or discussions. This will help reinforce what you are learning and help in the development of those around you.

Constant development should be a core value for a business. Everyone should be in the habit of learning and sharing what they know. This will help the company adopt new ideas and practices. As noted earlier, a company should have a physical or virtual library where employees can gain inspiration and knowledge.

Oprah is well known for inspiring countless people by sharing what she reads.[574] She is not the only one who shared what they were learning through reading. Let's return to our Founding Fathers for a moment.

Our Founding Fathers were prolific writers and created content for the benefit of others. I can imagine Franklin would have been a world-class blogger and Twitter user today. Franklin wrote about everything from chess to creating pro/con lists. These leaders were eager to learn and share what they learned. According to *The Jefferson Monticello*, Jefferson wrote approximately 19,000 letters and had over 21,000 letters written to him.[575] For forty-three years, he wrote at least four days of the week.[576] Franklin produced a newspaper, *The Pennsylvania Gazette*, and contributed to many other papers.[577]

John Adams documented his learning and journeys with a diary or journal. According to the Massachusetts Historical Society, Adams wrote fifty-one journal volumes from 1753 to 1804.[578]

I am not the only one who has realized our Founding Fathers were personal learning network rock stars. Others have imagined Jefferson cataloging his findings on a myriad of topics on Pinterest.[579] Franklin would be tweeting inspirational quotes, and Adams would be connecting on LinkedIn. Franklin believed in sharing knowledge and would use social media to do so.[580]

"His quest for useful knowledge and self-improvement flourished within the precincts of the study circle and subscription library, amid the mysteries of the local Masonic lodge, and inside the collegiality of the coffee klatsch, the tavern gathering, and the drinking club."[581]

Adams, Jefferson, and Franklin were always seeking out others to share knowledge. They did this in tavern gatherings and through the written word. Additionally, they were all curious and voracious readers.

Do not hoard the information learned when reading a good book. Instead, share knowledge with others through blogging, vlogging (video blogging), and discussion. Take time to teach others what you have learned. Finally, share what you are reading.

Blog What You Read

I have blogged for over six years about books I have read. If there is a specific group that would find the book useful, I included them in my post. As a bonus, I tied the books to Amazon's affiliate marketing program. It never hurts to make a couple of pennies. In this way, I can benefit on many fronts.

There are other ways to write in relation to what one reads besides book reviews:[582]

- Complete exercises recommended in the book and write about the experience.
- Write about a particular quote that resonated with you.

Teach Others

Teaching about what you read is one of the most beneficial actions you can do to help you remember what you've read.[583] Knowledge can be shared in face-to-face settings, on blogs, in videos, through podcasts, and in many other ways.

As noted earlier, leaders like Franklin, Patton, Adams, and Jefferson would meet with friends on a regular basis to share what they learned from their reading. They would discuss a book, take part in a book club, or give lectures.

Book Clubs

Book clubs get another mention here because they are great places to share what is learned from a book. Sometimes others need a little bit of encouragement to get started reading again. An invitation to join a book club may be the spark they need. Book clubs can be face-to-face or virtual.

Use Apps to Spread Reading Influence

I use two programs to share what I have read. Goodreads is the first. I use it to track what I am reading, follow what others are reading, and suggest books for others to read. BookCrossing is the other program I use to give away books and track their journey as strangers pick them up, read them, and release them back into the world.

Goodreads

At time of writing, the Goodreads platform boasted more than 50 million users. With Goodreads, you can track which books have been read, want to read, and are reading. You can also see books your friends share and get recommendations for new books to read.

Books can be entered many ways. Once entered, a book can be marked, rated, tagged, and a review added. I write my review on my blog, then copy the top paragraph and enter it into Goodreads with a link to my blog.

Goodreads also lets you see what your friends are reading and receive suggestions from them. You can also suggest books for them. I receive an email from Goodreads every day. It's a nice way to keep focused on reading and the power of reading.

BookCrossing

BookCrossing allows you to "release" your books "into the wild." If you've finished reading a book and don't wish to keep it in your library, you can share it with a stranger by leaving it in a place for others to find.

You can register the book with BookCrossing before releasing it. BookCrossing then assigns the book a number, which you add to a sticker that you place in the book. BookCrossing provides sample stickers to print and use. The result is a very open, global library. Book-Crossing encourages those who find books to log them with Book-Crossing. They should make a journal entry after reading a book and then release the book back into the wild.

I have left registered books on benches at colleges and bus stops.

Wrap Up

Reading is a great way to get information and build knowledge, but you should consider doing more with what you've learned. Share your knowledge with others through improved processes and procedures. As John F. Kennedy said, "The rising tide lifts all the boats." By sharing what is learned, you can help others improve. When everyone improves, operations will improve. You can also share what you learn by writing blog posts, teaching workshops, or having good old-fashioned discussions.

Teaching what you learn provides a better understanding. Everyone wins.

Final Thoughts

Congratulations! You now have a toolbox of techniques and strategies to develop a reading habit that will help you achieve higher levels of success. You should now have a better understanding of why you should be reading more, how to read better and more, where to find books to read as well as the time to read them, and when and where you should read.

Who knew there was so much involved in reading to succeed! Reading, like any other worthwhile activity, takes time to develop into a habit. But the benefits of reading are real, long lasting, and well worth it.

It is time for you to start your reading habit to success. Like other habits, it is important to start small. Start by establishing an achievable reading goal. Next, break the reading goal into small, actionable steps. Work these steps into your daily routine. As you become accustomed to this new activity in your life, you can then make it more challenging. For example, if you want to read a book every two weeks, you should start by establishing your baseline reading speed. Once you determine how many pages you can read per minute, you can then calculate how much time you need to dedicate per day to read a book. For example, if you read one page per minute and set aside fifteen minutes per day to read, you could read a two-hundred-page book in approximately two weeks. If you set aside thirty minutes to read each day, you could read a two-hundred-page book each week.

Join me on Goodreads! It's a great platform to share what you are reading, and it automatically tracks how many pages and books you have read. If you need motivation you can participate in a Goodreads reading challenge, in which you declare how many books you are planning to read and attempt to reach that goal.

Most importantly, start reading and improving your quality of life. As I have stressed throughout this book, reading will provide you with notable benefits. The ideas you will generate by listening to experts will show up in your work, play, and studies. You will experience higher levels of performance. Finally, share what you have learned with others. Help make the world a better place.

I wish you luck with your reading adventures and success!

About the Author

Stan Skrabut is a card-carrying lifelong learner who has spent his career helping people and organizations achieve improved performance. He is a scholar, teacher, veteran, martial artist, and avid reader. He has worked as a guard, organizational trainer, instructional technologist, webmaster, systems programmer, lecturer, and director. He uses informal learning, especially reading, as a way to improve himself and his teams. His interest in informal learning inspired his dissertation topic, *Study of Informal Learning among University of Wyoming Extension Educators.*

Stan Skrabut lives with his wife and two dogs in upstate New York. Nomadic in nature, he loves to travel and has lived in Germany, Belgium, the Netherlands, Turkey, and various locations across the United States. His number-one passion is helping others achieve their goals.

Bibliography

Ackoff, Russell, and Daniel Greenberg. *Turning Learning Right Side up: Putting Education Back on Track*. Upper Saddle River N.J.: Wharton School Pub., 2008.

Acuff, Jonathan M. *Start: Punch Fear in the Face, Escape Average, Do Work That Matters*. Brentwood, Tennessee: Lampo Press, 2013.

"Adams Electronic Archive : Diary of John Adams." Massachusetts Historical Society. Accessed May 20, 2016. http://www.masshist.org/digitaladams/archive/diary/.

Adler, Mortimer Jerome, and Charles Lincoln Van Doren. *How to Read a Book*. Rev. and updated ed. New York: Simon and Schuster, 1972.

Alber, Rebecca. "5 Reasons to Read for Reluctant Readers." Edutopia, April 28, 2016. http://www.edutopia.org/blog/5-reading-reasons-reluctant-readers-rebecca-alber.

Alter, Alexandra. "The Plot Twist: E-Book Sales Slip, and Print Is Far from Dead." *The New York Times*, September 22, 2015. http://www.nytimes.com/2015/09/23/business/media/the-plot-twist-e-book-sales-slip-and-print-is-far-from-dead.html.

Alves, David. "How to Build Your Personal Library." *David's Place* (blog), September 20, 2011. https://davidcalves.com/2011/09/20/how-to-build-your-personal-library/.

Ambler, George. "Reading Keeps Leaders Smart, Creative and Social." George Ambler, January 17, 2015. http://www.georgeambler.com/reading-keeps-leaders-smart-creative-social/.

American Antiquarian Society. "Personal Libraries: Washington." A Place of Reading, 2010. http://www.americanantiquarian.org/Exhibitions/Reading/washington.htm.

American Chemical Society. "Thomas Edison, Chemist." American Chemical Society, 2016. https://www.acs.org/content/acs/en/education/whatischemistry/landmarks/thomas-edison.html.

Amod, Sheraan. "10 Success Principles from Mark Cuban That Made Him Rich." Sheraan Amod | Blog, 2012. http://sheraan.com/post/19865115481/10-success-principles-from-mark-cuban-that-made.

Anderberg, Jeremy. "Theodore Roosevelt's Reading List." *The Art of Manliness* (blog), February 3, 2014. http://www.artofmanliness.com/2014/02/03/the-libraries-of-great-men-theodore-roosevelts-reading-list/.

Andrew Perrin. "Who Doesn't Read Books in America?" *Pew Research Center* (blog), March 23, 2018. http://www.pewresearch.org/fact-tank/2018/03/23/who-doesnt-read-books-in-america/.

AoM Team. "Books That Influenced Abraham Lincoln." *The Art of Manliness* (blog), September 15, 2015. http://www.artofmanliness.com/2015/09/15/the-libraries-of-famous-men-abraham-lincoln/.

Applegate, Anthony J., Mary DeKonty Applegate, Martha A. Mercantini, Catherine M. McGeehan, Jeanne B. Cobb, Joanne R. DeBoy, Virginia B. Modla, and Kimberly E. Lewinski. "The Peter Effect Revisited: Reading Habits and Attitudes of College Students." *Literacy Research and Instruction* 53, no. 3 (July 3, 2014): 188–204. https://doi.org/10.1080/19388071.2014.898719.

Attwell, Graham. "Web 2.0 and the Changing Ways We Are Using Computers for Learning: What Are the Implications for Pedagogy and Curriculum?," April 6, 2010. http://citeseerx.ist.psu.edu/viewdoc/download?doi=10.1.1.122.6064&rep=rep1&type=pdf.

Austin, Ben. "'Billionaire' Reading Habits: 11 Ways to Read 52 Books in 52 Weeks, 2X Your Reading Speed and Improve Your Comprehension by 500%." Stop. Start. Do. Accessed November 15, 2016. http://www.stopstartdo.com/blog/become-billionaire-smart-how-to-read-52-books-in-52-weeks.

Azulay, Halelly. "5 Ways to Develop Employees without Spending a Dime." Association for Talent Development, September 17, 2012. https://www.td.org/Publications/Blogs/Management-Blog/2012/09/5-Ways-to-Develop-Employees-Without-Spending-a-Dime.

Bahnck, Heidi. "How to Pick Books to Read." *Pro Book Club* (blog), May 1, 2014. http://probookclub.com/how-to-pick-books-to-read/.

Beals, Gerald. "Edison Biography." THomasEdison.com, 1999. http://www.thomasedison.com/biography.html.

Bell, Chip R. "Informal Learning in Organizations." *Personnel J*, no. 6 (1977): 280.

Belliveau, Vincent. "The Industrialisation of Informal Learning." *Training Journal*, 2010, 50–53.

"Benefits of Reading & Advantages of Reading a Book." Time2Change. Accessed July 17, 2016. https://selfhelpfix.com/benefits-of-reading.php.

Besse, Ralph M. "The Philosophy of Reading." Foundation for Economic Education, January 1, 1956. https://fee.org/articles/the-philosophy-of-reading/.

Bet-David, Patrick. "How to Choose the Right Books to Read." *Patrick Bet-David* (blog), September 13, 2016. http://www.patrickbetdavid.com/choose-the-right-books-to-read/.

Biography.com Editors. "Thomas Edison Biography." *The Biography.Com Website* (blog), February 5, 2016. http://www.biography.com/people/thomas-edison-9284349.

Birdsong, Jon. "5 Learnings from Abraham Lincoln before He Turned 40." *WideAngle* (blog), August 7, 2016. https://wideangle.com/blog/2016/08/learning-abraham-lincoln.

Birkett, Alex. "Think like a Rough Rider: Productivity Hacks from Teddy Roosevelt." The Roosevelts, September 22, 2014. http://www.rsvlts.com/2014/09/22/productivity-hacks-from-teddy-roosevelt/.

Bogel, Anne. "The 2016 Reading Challenge." Modern Mrs. Darcy, December 29, 2015. http://modernmrsdarcy.com/2016-reading-challenge/.

Bruce. "Career Hacks from Young George Washington." Project Management Hacks, March 10, 2015. http://projectmanagementhacks.com/career-hacks-young-george-washington/.

Burak, Lydia. "Examining and Predicting College Students' Reading Intentions and Behaviors: An Application of the Theory of Reasoned Action." *Reading Horizon* 45, no. 2 (December 2004): 139–53.

Burke, Crispin. "6 Smart Habits of the US Military's Most Successful Commanders." Task & Purpose, April 17, 2015. http://taskandpurpose.com/6-smart-habits-of-the-us-militarys-most-successful-commanders.

Byerly, Joe. "Use 'Mental Models' to Outthink the Enemy." Association of the United States Army, August 15, 2016. https://www.ausa.org/articles/use-%E2%80%98mental-models%E2%80%99-outthink-enemy.

Carroll, Ryder. "Bullet Journal." Bullet Journal, 2016. http://bulletjournal.com/.

CCC Foundation. "Building a Better Vocabulary." Capital Community College Foundation. Accessed November 2, 2016. http://grammar.ccc.commnet.edu/grammar/vocabulary.htm.

Chirravoori, Meghashyam. "Why the Reading Habit Is an Amazing Habit to Develop." Personal-Development-Is-Fun.com. Accessed November 20, 2016. http://www.personal-development-is-fun.com/the-reading-habit.html.

Chrystal, William. "What Is a Good Citizen? Thoughts from Some of the Founding Fathers." The Federalist Papers, May 18, 2013. http://thefederalistpapers.org/current-events/what-is-a-good-citizen-thoughts-from-some-of-the-founding-fathers.

"Close Reading." *Wikipedia*, November 15, 2017. https://en.wikipedia.org/w/index.php?title=Close_reading&oldid=810524411.

Coleman, John. "For Those Who Want to Lead, Read." Harvard Business Review, August 15, 2012. https://hbr.org/2012/08/for-those-who-want-to-lead-rea.

———. "Why Businesspeople Should Join Book Clubs." Harvard Business Review, February 23, 2016. https://hbr.org/2016/02/why-businesspeople-should-join-book-clubs.

Corley, Thomas C. "Reading and Success – a Simple Matter of Cause and Effect." Rich Habits Institute, April 17, 2014. http://richhabits.net/is-there-a-correlation-between-being-rich-and-reading-habits/.

———. "Reading Habits of the Affluent." Rich Habits Institute, May 13, 2014. http://richhabits.net/reading-habits-of-the-rich-what-the-wealthy-read/.

Cornell College. "How to Read Closely: Making Sense out of Novels." Cornell College. Accessed November 5, 2016. http://www.cornellcollege.edu/academic-support-and-advising/study-tips/reading-closely.shtml.

Corrigan, Paul. "Students, Keep Your Books." Inside Higher Ed, June 3, 2016. https://www.insidehighered.com/views/2016/06/03/enduring-power-textbooks-students-lives-essay.

Cortes, Tony. "Invest Learn Teach - Powerful Method to Build Authority." *Tony Cortes* (blog), February 2, 2016. http://www.tonycortes.com/invest-learn-teach/.

Cothran, Martin. "The Classical Education of the Founding Fathers." Memoria Press, April 15, 2007. https://www.memoriapress.com/articles/classical-education-founding-fathers/.

Cottrell, David. *Tuesday Morning Coaching: Eight Simple Truths to Boost Your Career and Your Life*. New York: McGraw-Hill, 2013.

Cross, Jay. *Informal Learning: Rediscovering the Natural Pathways That Inspire Innovation and Performance*. San Francisco, CA: John Wiley & Sons, Inc., 2007.

Cunningham, Anne, and Keith Stanovich. "What Reading Does for the Mind." *American Educator/American Federation of Teachers* Spring/Summer (1998): 1–8.

Curry, Kevin. "Learn from the Reading Habits of Successful People." ZipRage, April 20, 2016. https://ziprage.com/learn-from-the-reading-habits-of-successful-people/.

D'Aprile, Jason. "In Defense of the E-Reader." *Tech50+* (blog), August 22, 2016. https://tech50plus.com/in-defense-of-the-e-reader/.

Davis, Glenn. "Why Is Reading Important?" Learn To Read, December 2014. http://www.learn-to-read-prince-george.com/why-is-reading-important.html.

Day, Nancy. "Informal Learning Gets Results." *Workforce* 77, no. 6 (June 1998): 30–36.

Deering, Ron. "Ray Higdons ILT Method for Blogging • Ron Deering." *Ron Deering* (blog), March 9, 2015. https://rondeering.com/ray-higdons-ilt-method-for-blogging/.

Dillon, Andrew. "Reading from Paper versus Screens: A Critical Review of the Empirical Literature." *Ergonomics* 35, no. 10 (October 1992): 1297–1326. https://doi.org/10.1080/00140139208967394.

"Dolly Parton's Imagination Library," 2018. https://imaginationlibrary.com/.

Dooley, Erin. "Here's Obama's Childhood Reading List." ABC News, May 1, 2015. http://abcnews.go.com/Politics/president-obama-childhood-reading-list/story?id=30703821.

Douglas, Jonathan. "The Importance of Instilling a Need to Read." *The Telegraph*, May 4, 2013, sec. Education. http://www.telegraph.co.uk/education/educationopinion/10035473/The-importance-of-instilling-a-need-to-read.html.

Dublin, Lance. "Formalizing Informal Learning." *Chief Learning Officer* 9, no. 3 (2010): 20–23.

"Edisonian Approach." *Wikipedia*, September 12, 2017. https://en.wikipedia.org/w/index.php?title=Edisonian_approach&oldid=800292477.

Edmonds, Molly. "How to Create a Home Library." HowStuffWorks, March 24, 2008. http://home.howstuffworks.com/home-improvement/remodeling/home-library.htm.

Elkins, Kathleen. "A Self-Made Millionaire Who Studied 1,200 Wealthy People Found They All Have One — Free — Pastime in Common," August 21, 2015. http://www.businessinsider.com/rich-people-like-to-read-2015-8.

Empact. "Why Constant Learners All Embrace the 5-Hour Rule." Inc.com, June 20, 2016. http://www.inc.com/empact/why-constant-learners-all-embrace-the-5-hour-rule.html.

Encyclopedia.com. "Patton, George S. - Dictionary Definition of Patton, George S. |
    Encyclopedia.Com: FREE Online Dictionary." Accessed October 29, 2016.
    http://www.encyclopedia.com/history/educational-magazines/patton-george-s.

Evans, Harold. "White House Book Club." The New Yorks Times, January 14,
    2001. http://www.nytimes.com/books/01/01/14/bookend/bookend.html.

Feldman, Richard. "Speed Reading: 10 Tips to Improve Reading Speed & Compre-
    hension." Learning Techniques, 2015. http://www.learningtechniques.com/
    speedreadingtips.html.

Ferriss, Tim. "General Stan McChrystal on Eating One Meal per Day, Special Ops,
    and Mental Toughness." The Tim Ferriss Show (blog), July 5, 2015. http://
    fourhourworkweek.com/2015/07/05/stanley-mcchrystal/.

———. "Scientific Speed Reading: How to Read 300% Faster in 20 Minutes." The
    Time Ferriss Show (blog), July 30, 2009. http://
    fourhourworkweek.com/2009/07/30/speed-reading-and-accelerated-learning/.

Ferriss, Timothy. Tools of Titans: The Tactics, Routines, and Habits of Billionaires,
    Icons, and World-Class Performers. Boston: Houghton Mifflin Harcourt, 2016.

Flood, Alison. "President Obama Says Novels Taught Him 'the Most Important'
    Things about Being a Citizen." RawStory, October 28, 2015. http://
    www.rawstory.com/2015/10/president-obama-says-novels-taught-him-the-most
    -important-things-about-being-a-citizen/.

Foasberg, Nancy M. "Adoption of E-Book Readers among College Students: A Sur-
    vey." Information Technology and Libraries 30, no. 3 (September 2, 2011).
    http://ejournals.bc.edu/ojs/index.php/ital/article/view/1769.

Fogleman, Ronald R. "CSAF Professional Reading Program." Airpower Journal 11,
    no. 1 (Spring 1997): 63–65.

Ford, Mark Morgan. "An Idea for You from Bill Gates That Will Help You Take a
    Giant Step Forward." Early To Rise (blog), April 4, 2005. http://
    www.earlytorise.com/an-idea-for-you-from-bill-gates-that-will-help-you-take-a-
    giant-step-forward/.

Franklin, Benjamin, and E. Boyd (Elmer Boyd) Smith. Autobiography of Benjamin
    Franklin. Edited by Frank Woodworth Pine, 2006. http://www.gutenberg.org/
    ebooks/20203.

"Franklin D. Roosevelt." Wikipedia, December 23, 2017. https://en.wikipedia.org/
    w/index.php?title=Franklin_D._Roosevelt&oldid=816761211.

French, Leah. "How to Create a Home Library Using Flea Market Finds." The

Spruce. Accessed October 7, 2018. https://www.thespruce.com/how-to-create-a
-home-library-1313432.

Fuller, Jaime. "BREAKING: President Obama Hates Cable News." Washington
Post, September 26, 2014. https://www.washingtonpost.com/news/the-fix/
wp/2014/09/26/breaking-president-obama-hates-cable-news/.

Gelman, Lauren. "Benefits of Reading: Getting Smart, Thin, Healthy, Happy."
Reader's Digest, September 9, 2013. http://www.rd.com/health/wellness/
benefits-of-reading/.

"George Patton." DyslexiaHelp, 2016. http://dyslexiahelp.umich.edu/success-
stories/george-patton.

Gilbert, J., and B. Fister. "Reading, Risk, and Reality: College Students and Reading
for Pleasure." *College & Research Libraries* 72, no. 5 (September 1, 2011): 474–
95. https://doi.org/10.5860/crl-148.

Gilmore, Agatha. "Hands off: Facilitating Informal Learning." *Certification Magazine* 10, no. 10 (2008): 46–49.

Gladu, Alex. "Why Reading a Print Book Is Better for You and for Main Street."
Independent We Stand, May 10, 2016. http://www.independentwestand.org/
blog-reading-a-print-book-is-better-for-you/.

Goins, Jeff. "083: How to Build Better Reading Habits and Finish a Book Every
Day." Goins, Writer, December 2, 2015. http://goinswriter.com/read-books/.

Goo, Sara Kehaulani. "The Skills Americans Say Kids Need to Succeed in Life." *Pew
Research Center* (blog), February 19, 2015. http://www.pewresearch.org/fact-
tank/2015/02/19/skills-for-success/.

Grant, Alexis. "11 Ways to Take Notes While Reading." *Real-Time Chat for Online
Hiring & Networking* (blog), April 28, 2010. http://www.brazen.com/blog/
archive/smart-hacks/11-ways-to-take-notes-while-reading/.

Grate, Rachel. "Science Has Great News for People Who Read Actual Books."
Arts.Mic, September 22, 2014. https://mic.com/articles/99408/science-has-
great-news-for-people-who-read-actual-books.

Greene, Jackie, and Linda Serro. "Encouraging Critical Thinking and Professional
Reading with Literacy Bags." *The Open Communication Journal* 9, no. Supp11:
M10 (2015): 65–71.

Greer, Jim. "Want More Military Leaders Reading? Use the Pabst Blue Ribbon
Strategy." *From the Green Notebook* (blog), July 16, 2015. https://
fromthegreennotebook.com/2015/07/16/want-more-military-leaders-reading-

use-the-pabst-blue-ribbon-strategy/.

Grier, Peter. "John F. Kennedy: Why Books Were a Big Part of His Life." *Christian Science Monitor*, November 23, 2013. http://www.csmonitor.com/USA/Politics/Decoder/2013/1123/John-F.-Kennedy-Why-books-were-a-big-part-of-his-life-video.

Grothaus, Michael. "How Changing Your Reading Habits Can Transform Your Health." Fast Company, July 27, 2015. http://www.fastcompany.com/3048913/how-to-be-a-success-at-everything/how-changing-your-reading-habits-can-transform-your-health.

Gulledge, Jacqueline. "Dolly Parton's Mission to End Illiteracy." CNN, November 3, 2016. http://www.cnn.com/2016/11/02/entertainment/iyw-dolly-parton-imagination-library/index.html.

Ha, Thu-Huong. "Barack Obama Says He Learned How to Be a Good Citizen from Reading Novels." *Quartz* (blog), October 27, 2015. http://qz.com/534165/barack-obama-says-he-learned-how-to-be-a-good-citizen-from-reading-novels/.

Hansen, Katherine. "10 Ways to Build Your Vocabulary." MyCollegeSuccessStory.com. Accessed October 29, 2016. http://www.mycollegesuccessstory.com/academic-success-tools/build-vocabulary.html.

Hansen, Randall. "Easy Ways to Improve and Expand Your Vocabulary." EnhanceMyVocabulary.com. Accessed October 29, 2016. http://www.enhancemyvocabulary.com/improve-expand-vocabulary.html.

Harpham, Bruce. "9 Can't-Miss Secrets behind Warren Buffett's Wealth." Lifehack. Accessed October 26, 2016. http://www.lifehack.org/articles/money/9-cant-miss-secrets-behind-warren-buffetts-wealth.html.

———. "16 Skills To Make Your Reading More Productive." LifeHack. Accessed October 6, 2018. https://www.lifehack.org/articles/productivity/16-skills-make-your-reading-more-productive.html.

Harrington, Walt. "Dubya and Me." The American Scholar, August 25, 2011. https://theamericanscholar.org/dubya-and-me/#.

Heap, Kris. "The 8 Amazing Habits of Abraham Lincoln." *Successify!* (blog), March 28, 2013. http://successify.net/2013/03/28/the-8-amazing-habits-of-abraham-lincoln/.

Hernandez, Donald. "Double Jeopardy: How Third-Grade Reading Skills and Poverty Influence High School Graduation." University at Albany, State University of New York: The Annie E. Casey Foundation, April 2011. https://www.fcd-us.org/assets/2016/04/DoubleJeopardyReport.pdf.

Holiday, Ryan. "How and Why to Keep a 'Commonplace Book.'" *Thought Catalog* (blog), August 28, 2013. http://thoughtcatalog.com/ryan-holiday/2013/08/how-and-why-to-keep-a-commonplace-book/.

———. "How to Keep a Library of (Physical) Books." *Thought Catalog* (blog), September 17, 2013. http://thoughtcatalog.com/ryan-holiday/2013/09/how-to-keep-a-library-of-physical-books/.

———. "The Notecard System: The Key for Remembering, Organizing and Using Everything You Read." RyanHoliday.net, April 1, 2014. http://ryanholiday.net/the-notecard-system-the-key-for-remembering-organizing-and-using-everything-you-read/.

Honan, William H. "Books, Books and More Books: Clinton an Omnivorous Reader." *The New York Times*, December 10, 1992, sec. Books. http://www.nytimes.com/1992/12/10/books/books-books-and-more-books-clinton-an-omnivorous-reader.html.

Huang, SuHua, Matthew Capps, Jeff Blacklock, and Mary Garza. "Reading Habits of College Students in the United States." *Reading Psychology* 35, no. 5 (July 4, 2014): 437–67. https://doi.org/10.1080/02702711.2012.739593.

Hyatt, Michael. "5 Ways Reading Makes You a Better Leader." Michael Hyatt, May 4, 2015. http://michaelhyatt.com/science-readers-leaders.html.

Ingersoll, Geoffrey. "General James 'Mad Dog' Mattis Email about Being 'Too Busy to Read' Is a Must-Read." Business Insider, May 9, 2013. http://www.businessinsider.com/viral-james-mattis-email-reading-marines-2013-5.

Isaac, Brad. "5 Sneaky and Underhanded Methods to Add 30% More Time to Your Daily Reading Schedule." Persistence Unlimited, December 14, 2007. http://www.persistenceunlimited.com/2007/12/5-sneaky-and-underhanded-methods-to-add-30-more-time-to-your-daily-reading-schedule/.

———. "The 26 Major Advantages to Reading More Books and Why 3 in 4 People Are Being Shut out of Success." Persistence Unlimited, December 5, 2007. http://www.persistenceunlimited.com/2007/12/the-26-major-advantages-to-reading-more-books-and-why-3-in-4-people-are-being-shut-out-of-success/.

Jabr, Ferris. "The Reading Brain in the Digital Age: The Science of Paper versus Screens." Scientific American, April 11, 2013. https://www.scientificamerican.com/article/reading-paper-screens/.

Jenkins, Simon. "Books Are Back. Only the Technodazzled Thought They Would

Go Away." *The Guardian*, May 13, 2016, sec. Opinion. https://
www.theguardian.com/commentisfree/2016/may/13/books-ebook-publishers-paper.

John F. Kennedy biography. "John F. Kennedy Biography - Life, Family, Childhood, Children, Death, History, Wife, School, Mother." Encyclopedia of World Biographies. Accessed November 12, 2016. http://www.notablebiographies.com/Jo-Ki/Kennedy-John-F.html.

Johnson O'Connor Research Foundation. "Effective Ways to Build Your Vocabulary." Johnson O'Connor Research Foundation. Accessed November 1, 2016. http://www.jocrf.org/resources/effective-ways-build-your-vocabulary.

Juma, Aly. "What Is a Commonplace Book & Why You Need One." Aly Juma, October 8, 2015. http://alyjuma.com/commonplace-book/.

Kane, Libby. "What Rich People Have next to Their Beds." Business Insider, June 17, 2014. http://www.businessinsider.com/rich-people-read-self-improvement-books-2014-6.

Keane, David. "Read Your Way to Success." The Art of Deliberate Success, December 1, 2014. http://artofdeliberatesuccess.com/blog/read-your-way-to-success/.

Kelly, Kevin. *The Inevitable: Understanding the 12 Technological Forces That Will Shape Our Future*. New York, New York: Viking, 2016.

King, Laiza. "6 Practical Tips to Help You Cultivate a Reading Habit." *Huffington Post* (blog), June 6, 2016. http://www.huffingtonpost.com/laiza-king-/6-practical-tips-to-help-_b_10311094.html.

Kinnison, Kendra. "How John F. Kennedy Used Discipline and Creativity to Become President." *Coach Kendra* (blog), August 3, 2012. http://kendrakinnison.com/john-f-kennedy/.

Klosowski, Thorin. "The Truth about Speed Reading." Lifehacker, March 13, 2014. http://lifehacker.com/the-truth-about-speed-reading-1542508398.

Kniffel, Leonard. "Reading for Life: Oprah Winfrey." ilovelibraries, August 10, 2011. http://www.ilovelibraries.org/article/reading-life-oprah-winfrey.

Knowles, Malcolm. *The Modern Practice of Adult Education: From Pedagogy to Andragogy*. Rev. and Updated. Wilton, Conn. ;Chicago, Ill: Association Press; Follett Pub. Co., 1980.

Konnikova, Maria. "Being a Better Online Reader." The New Yorker, July 16, 2014. http://www.newyorker.com/science/maria-konnikova/being-a-better-online-reader.

Korpelainen, Eija, and Mari Kira. "Employees' Choices in Learning How to Use Information and Communication Technology Systems at Work: Strategies and Approaches." *International Journal of Training and Development* 14, no. 1 (March 2010): 32–53. https://doi.org/10.1111/j.1468-2419.2009.00339.x.

La Rosa, Erin. "12 Scientific Ways Reading Can Actually Improve Your Life." BuzzFeed, June 7, 2013. http://www.buzzfeed.com/erinlarosa/12-scientific-ways-reading-can-actually-improve-your-life.

Latumahina, Donald. "How Business Leaders Read." *Life Optimizer* (blog), January 26, 2008. http://www.lifeoptimizer.org/2008/01/25/reading-tips-how-business-leaders-read/.

"Letter from John Adams to Abigail Adams, Post 12 May 1780." Accessed November 11, 2016. https://www.masshist.org/digitaladams/archive/doc?id=L17800512jasecond.

Levin, Heather. "How to Read More Books: Benefits of Reading." *Money Crashers* (blog), October 1, 2012. http://www.moneycrashers.com/read-more-books-benefits/.

Lim, Shawn. "Why Do You Need to Read Books and the Benefits of It." *Stunning Motivation* (blog), June 23, 2016. http://stunningmotivation.com/why-need-read-books-benefits/.

Lin, Judy. "10 Questions for Abraham Lincoln Scholar Ronald C. White Jr." UCLA Newsroom, February 12, 2009. http://newsroom.ucla.edu/stories/10-questions-for-abraham-lincoln-81493.

Linker 2. "Successful People and Their Reading Habits." Crossroads Staffing Services, August 5, 2016. http://www.crossroadsstaffing.com/blog/2016_08_05.html.

Looney, J. Jefferson. "Number of Letters Jefferson Wrote." The Jefferson Monticello, March 24, 2008. https://www.monticello.org/site/research-and-collections/number-letters-jefferson-wrote.

Lovelace, Alexander. "Patton's Last Command." Warfare History Network, September 13, 2016. http://warfarehistorynetwork.com/daily/wwii/pattons-last-command/.

Lyons, Jonathan. "Benjamin Franklin: America's First Social Networker?" *Science Friday* (blog), July 4, 2013. http://www.sciencefriday.com/articles/benjamin-franklin-americas-first-social-networker/.

Maher, John. "Audiobook Revenue Jumped 22.7% in 2018." PublishersWeekly.com, June 21, 2018. https://www.publishersweekly.com/pw/by-topic/industry-news/audio-books/article/77303-audiobook-revenue-jumped-22-7-in-2018.html.

Mandel, Seth. "The Silly Plan to Draft Gen. Mattis Shows What's Wrong with GOP." *New York Post* (blog), April 26, 2016. http://nypost.com/2016/04/25/the-silly-plan-to-draft-gen-mattis-shows-whats-wrong-with-gop/.

Manning, Katherine. "John Adams and His Classical Heritage." Accessed November 15, 2016. http://college.holycross.edu/faculty/wziobro/ClassicalAmerica/johnadams.htm.

Marine Corps Association & Foundation. "MCA&F's Unit Libraries: 'Giving the Marine a "No Excuse" Opportunity to Complete Their Reading.'" Marine Corps Association & Foundation, January 8, 2016. https://www.mcafdn.org/gallery/mcafs-unit-libraries-giving-marine-no-excuse-opportunity-complete-their-reading.

Marsick, Victoria, and Karen Watkins. *Informal and Incidental Learning in the Workplace.* London;New York: Routledge, 1990.

Martin, Carolyn. "Reading Has Changed in America." Cornell University New Student Reading Project. Accessed July 17, 2016. http://reading.cornell.edu/reading_project_06/gatsby/project.htm.

Mathew, Rajiv. "9 Things to Learn from Elon Musk." *CitizenTekk* (blog), November 21, 2013. http://www.citizentekk.com/elon-musk-qualities/.

McChrystal, General Stanley. *My Share of the Task: A Memoir.* Reprint edition. Portfolio Trade, 2014.

McChrystal, Stan. "How I Keep up with an Unrelenting Work Pace." LinkedIn Pulse, February 1, 2016. https://www.linkedin.com/pulse/my-life-outside-work-how-i-keep-up-unrelenting-pace-stan-mcchrystal.

McCormick, Jean. "Would Thomas Jefferson Have Tweeted?" BraveNew, October 17, 2013. https://bravenew.com/blog/2013/10/17/would-thomas-jefferson-have-tweeted/.

McKay, Brett. "George Patton Letter to His Son." *The Art of Manliness* (blog), August 21, 2011. http://www.artofmanliness.com/2011/08/21/manvotional-a-letter-from-general-george-s-patton-to-his-son/.

———. "How to Build Your Vocabulary in 5 Easy Steps." *The Art of Manliness* (blog), October 3, 2012. http://www.artofmanliness.com/2012/10/03/the-importance-of-building-your-vocabulary-and-5-easy-steps-to-doing-it/.

———. "How to Speed Read Like Theodore Roosevelt." *The Art of Manliness* (blog), October 18, 2009. http://www.artofmanliness.com/2009/10/18/how-to -speed-read-like-theodore-roosevelt/.

McLean, Scott. "Learning on the Margins of Adult Education: Self-Help Reading about Health, Relationships, and Career Success." *Studies in the Education of Adults* 46, no. 1 (April 30, 2014): 4–22.

Medved, Michael. "Obama's Revealing Book Bag." The Daily Beast, August 23, 2011. http://www.thedailybeast.com/articles/2011/08/23/obama-s-fictional- world-a-peek-at-his-vacation-reading-list.html.

Merle, Andrew. "The Reading Habits of Ultra-Successful People." The Huffington Post, April 16, 2016. http://www.huffingtonpost.com/andrew-merle/the- reading-habits-of-ult_b_9688130.html.

Meyer, Kelsey. "Why Leaders Must Be Readers." Forbes, August 3, 2012. http:// www.forbes.com/sites/85broads/2012/08/03/why-leaders-must-be-readers/ #483f766d6563.

"Millennials Want to Make Books Cool Again." *Fortune* (blog), June 7, 2016. http://fortune.com/2016/06/07/millennials-physical-books/.

Miller, Carolyn, Kristen Purcell, and Lee Rainie. "Reading Habits in Different Com- munities." Washington, D.C.: Pew Research Center's Internet & American Life Project, December 20, 2012. http://libraries.pewinternet.org/files/legacy-pdf/ LibrariesAndReading_CommunityTypes_12.20.12.pdf.

Miller, Jamie. "8 Ways I Use My Bullet Journal as a Reader & a Blogger." The Per- petual Page-Turner, September 2, 2016. http:// www.perpetualpageturner.com/2016/09/8-ways-i-use-my-bullet-journal-as-a- reader-a-blogger.html.

Miller, Justin. "How to Read 52 Books in 52 Weeks and Save Yourself $21,000." Lifehack. Accessed July 23, 2016. http://www.lifehack.org/articles/lifestyle/how -to-read-52-books-in-52-weeks-and-save-yourself-21000.html.

Milligan, Jonathan. "A Simple Guide to Indexing the Books You Read for Evernote." JonathanMilligan.com, June 4, 2014. http://jonathanmilligan.com/a- simple-guide-to-indexing-the-books-you-read-for-evernote/.

Mumford, Tracy. "A Bookish Tour through Obama's Years in the White House," January 19, 2017. http://www.mprnews.org/story/2017/01/19/books-obama- years-book-tour.

Myrberg, Caroline, and Ninna Wiberg. "Screen vs. Paper: What Is the Difference for Reading and Learning?" *Insights* 28, no. 2 (July 7, 2015). https://doi.org/10.1629/uksg.236.

myReadSpeed.com. "Calculate Your Reading Speed." myReadSpeed.com, 2009. http://www.myreadspeed.com/articles/calculate/.

Niccoli, Anne. "Paper or Tablet? Reading Recall and Comprehension." *EDUCAUSE Review*, September 28, 2015. http://er.educause.edu/articles/2015/9/paper-or-tablet-reading-recall-and-comprehension.

"Note-Taking for Reading." Skills You Need. Accessed September 17, 2016. http://www.skillsyouneed.com/write/notes-reading.html.

Oppong, Thomas. "This Is The Daily Routine of Warren Buffett," July 9, 2014. http://alltopstartups.com/2014/07/09/daily-routine-of-warren-buffett/.

Page, Susan. "Ronald Reagan's Note Card Collection Being Published." USATODAY.COM, May 8, 2011. http://www.usatoday.com/news/washington/2011-05-08-reagan-notes-book-brinkley_n.htm.

Parrish, Shane. "George Washington's Practical Self-Education." Farnam Street, June 13, 2016. https://www.farnamstreetblog.com/2016/06/george-washington-self-education/.

———. "Jeff Bezos's Reading List." The Week, October 22, 2013. http://theweek.com/articles/458345/jeff-bezoss-reading-list.

———. "The Best Way to Find More Time to Read." Farnam Street, September 2, 2013. https://www.farnamstreetblog.com/2013/09/finding-time-to-read/.

———. "The Top 3 Most Effective Ways to Take Notes While Reading." Farnam Street, November 26, 2013. https://www.farnamstreetblog.com/2013/11/taking-notes-while-reading/.

———. "What You Didn't Know about the Act of Reading Books." *Time*, August 24, 2015. http://time.com/3993897/schopenhauer-reading-books/.

Patrick, Tim. "Keeping up with the Jeffersons." *Well-Read Man* (blog), July 14, 2011. http://wellreadman.com/2011/07/14/keeping-up-with-jefferson/.

Pellot, Emerald. "Dolly Parton's Imagination Library Program Donates Books to Children to Promote Literacy." LittleThings.com. Accessed November 4, 2016. http://www.littlethings.com/dolly-parton-imagination-library/.

Pipes, Taylor. "Taking Note: What Commonplace Books Can Teach Us about Our Past." *Evernote Blog* (blog), February 26, 2016. https://blog.evernote.com/blog/2016/02/26/taking-note-what-commonplace-books-can-teach-us-about-our-past/.

———. "Timeless Note-Taking Systems for Students." *Evernote Blog* (blog), July 7, 2016. https://evernote.com/blog/timeless-note-taking-systems-for-students/.

Postolovski, Natasha. "The Transformative Effects of Reading + Elon Musk's Reading List." Inside Envato, January 21, 2015. http://inside.envato.com/the-transformative-effects-of-reading-elon-musks-reading-list/.

Powell, Jim. "The Education of Thomas Edison." Foundation for Economic Education, February 1, 1995. https://fee.org/articles/the-education-of-thomas-edison/.

Price, Tirzah. "Cool Bookish Ideas for Your Bullet Journal." *BOOK RIOT* (blog), August 11, 2016. http://bookriot.com/2016/08/11/cool-bookish-ideas-bullet-journal/.

Prindle, Beth, ed. "John Adams Unbound." American Library Association, 2008. http://www.ala.org/programming/sites/ala.org.programming/files/content/adams/files/34%2520Exhibit%2520script.doc.

Rainie, Lee. "7 Surprises about Libraries in Our Surveys." *Pew Research Center* (blog), June 30, 2014. http://www.pewresearch.org/fact-tank/2014/06/30/7-surprises-about-libraries-in-our-surveys/.

Rainie, Lee, Kathryn Zickuhr, Kristen Purcell, Mary Madden, and Joanna Brenner. "The Rise of E-Reading." *Pew Internet Libraries* (blog), 2012. http://libraries.pewinternet.org/2012/04/04/the-rise-of-e-reading/.

Rao, Srinivas. "How to Read 100 Books in a Year." The Mission, October 13, 2016. https://medium.com/the-mission/how-to-read-100-books-in-a-year-d7b35660ebd1#.v4mqicf1u.

"Readers Are Leaders: J.N. Whiddon's Tips to Reading 25 Books in a Year." PRWeb, March 24, 2016. http://www.prweb.com/releases/2016/03/prweb13266863.htm.

"Reading a Textbook for True Understanding." Cornell College. Accessed October 16, 2016. http://www.cornellcollege.edu/academic-support-and-advising/study-tips/reading-textbooks.shtml.

"Reading Habits: Leaders Are Learners." Dawn, June 11, 2011. http://www.dawn.com/2011/06/11/reading-habits-leaders-are-learners/.

Redden, Molly. "7 in 10 Students Have Skipped Buying a Textbook Because of Its Cost." The Chronicle of Higher Education, August 23, 2011. http://www.chronicle.com/article/7-in-10-Students-Have-Skipped/128785/.

Rove, Karl. "Bush Is a Book Lover." *Wall Street Journal*, December 26, 2008, sec.

Opinion. http://www.wsj.com/articles/SB123025595706634689.

Rubin, Harriet. "C.E.O. Libraries Reveal Keys to Success." *The New York Times*, July 21, 2007. http://www.nytimes.com/2007/07/21/business/21libraries.html.

Sanderson, Jeffrey. "General George S. Patton Jr.: Master of Operational Battle Command. What Lasting Battle Command Lessons Can We Learn from Him?" School of Advanced Military Studies, United States Army Command and General Staff College, May 22, 1997. http://www.dtic.mil/dtic/tr/fulltext/u2/a331356.pdf.

Schawbel, Dan. "General Stanley McChrystal: Leadership Lessons from Afghanistan." Forbes, January 10, 2013. http://www.forbes.com/sites/danschawbel/2013/01/10/general-stanley-mcchrystal-leadership-lessons-from-afghanistan/.

Shackleton-Jones, Nick. "Informal Learning and the Future." *Training Journal*, 2008, 38–41.

Shear, Michael D. "Obama after Dark: The Precious Hours Alone." *The New York Times*, July 2, 2016. http://www.nytimes.com/2016/07/03/us/politics/obama-after-dark-the-precious-hours-alone.html.

Siemens, George. *Knowing Knowledge*. Lexington, KY, 2006. http://www.elearnspace.org/KnowingKnowledge_LowRes.pdf.

Simmons, Michael. "9 Creative Ways to Find Books That Will Make You a Genius." Forbes, September 24, 2015. http://www.forbes.com/sites/michaelsimmons/2015/09/24/9-creative-ways-to-find-books-that-will-make-you-a-genius/#15d7db892c47.

Skrabut, Stan. "A Study of Informal Learning Among University of Wyoming Extension Educators." University of Wyoming, 2013.

Smallwood, Karl. "Theodore Roosevelt Could Read a Book before Breakfast." *Fact Fiend* (blog), July 15, 2014. http://www.factfiend.com/theodore-roosevelt-read-book-breakfast/.

Stager, Gary. "Everything I Know about Reading Instruction I Learned from Oprah Winfrey." *Gary S. Stager* (blog), n.d. http://www.stager.org/articles/oprah.html.

Stansberry, Glen. "Benefits of Reading: 8 Reasons Books Improve Your Life." LifeDev, December 17, 2014. http://lifedev.net/2009/06/reading-makes-you-better/.

Staton-Reinstein, Rebecca. "Why Successful Business Leaders Love History." ReliablePlant. Accessed November 13, 2016. http://reliableplant.com/Read/13569/why-successful-business-leaders-love-history.

Stillman, Jessica. "Mark Zuckerberg and President Obama Both Read Fiction (You Should Too)." Inc.com, November 2, 2015. http://www.inc.com/jessica-stillman/why-mark-zuckerberg-likes-to-kick-back-with-a-page-turner-and-why-you-should-too.html.

———. "Yet Another Reason You Should Read More: You'll Live Longer." Inc.com, August 23, 2016. http://www.inc.com/jessica-stillman/yet-another-reason-you-should-read-more-youll-live-longer.html.

Strauss, Valerie. "Most Literate Nation in the World? Not the U.S., New Ranking Says." Washington Post, March 8, 2016. https://www.washingtonpost.com/news/answer-sheet/wp/2016/03/08/most-literate-nation-in-the-world-not-the-u-s-new-ranking-says/.

Sturgeon, Jonathon. "Reading Habits of the Rich and Powerful, 2016 Edition: Gates, Zuckerberg, Obama." *Flavorwire* (blog), January 7, 2016. http://flavorwire.com/554696/reading-habits-of-the-rich-and-powerful-2016-edition-gates-zuckerberg-obama.

Sviokla, John, and Mitch Cohen. "Mark Cuban Used to Stay up All Night Reading about Stamps." Business Insider, January 7, 2015. http://www.businessinsider.com/mark-cuban-baseball-cards-2015-1.

Swanson, Kristen. *Professional Learning in the Digital Age: The Educator's Guide to User-Generated Learning.* Larchmont, NY: Eye on Education, 2013.

Talbert, Robert. "Teddy Roosevelt's to-Do List." Casting Out Nines, August 18, 2008. https://castingoutnines.wordpress.com/2008/08/18/teddy-roosevelts-to-do-list/.

Tanner, M. "Digital vs. Print: Reading Comprehension and the Future of the Book." *SJSU School of Information Student Research Journal* 4, no. 2 (December 19, 2014). http://scholarworks.sjsu.edu/slissrj/vol4/iss2/6.

Tay, Endrina. "Jefferson, Thomas and Books." Encyclopedia Virginia, November 21, 2016. http://www.encyclopediavirginia.org/Jefferson_Thomas_and_Books.

"The Best-Read Presidents." The Daily Beast, February 14, 2010. http://www.thedailybeast.com/galleries/2010/02/14/the-best-read-presidents.html.

The Lieutenant. "5 Life Lessons from JFK." *Return of the Kings* (blog), December 6, 2013. http://www.returnofkings.com/22635/5-life-lessons-from-jfk.

The Literacy Company. "Some Well-Known Speed Readers." The Literacy Company, 2016. http://www.readfaster.com/articles/well-known-speed-readers.asp.

The Training Doctor. "Reading Teaches Thinking Skills." *The Training Doctor* (blog), February 26, 2016. http://www.trainingdr.com/reading-teaches-thinking-skills/.

"The U.S. Army Chief of Staff Professional Reading List." U.S. Army Center of Military History, n.d. http://www.history.army.mil/html/books/105/105-1-1/CMH_Pub_105-5-1_2013.pdf.

thepower. "Thomas Edison's and His Struggles with Dyslexia." *The Power of Dyslexia* (blog), 2012. http://thepowerofdyslexia.com/thomas-edison/.

"Third-Grade Reading Legislation." NCSL: National Conference of State Legislatures, May 23, 2018. http://www.ncsl.org/research/education/third-grade-reading-legislation.aspx.

Thomas Edison Center. "Thomas Edison and Menlo Park." *Thomas Edison Center at Menlo Park* (blog), 2009. http://www.menloparkmuseum.org/history/thomas-edison-and-menlo-park/.

Thomas, Suneel. "Elon Musk's Secret Sauce to Grow at 10x Speed." Techachari, July 9, 2015. http://www.techachari.com/grow-10x-speed/.

Thorne, Ashley. "Students Will Rise When Colleges Challenge Them to Read Good Books." The Chronicle of Higher Education, March 13, 2016. http://chronicle.com/article/Students-Will-Rise-When/235681/.

Tobin, Daniel. *All Learning Is Self-Directed: How Organizations Can Support and Encourage Independent Learning.* Alexandria VA: ASTD, 2000.

Tough, Allen. *Intentional Changes: A Fresh Approach to Helping People Change.* Chicago Ill.: Follett Pub. Co., 1982.

Tough, Allen M. *Why Adults Learn: A Study of the Major Reasons for Beginning and Continuing a Learning Project.* Toronto: Ontario Inst. for Studies in Education, 1968. http://search.ebscohost.com.proxy.uwlib.uwyo.edu/login.aspx?direct=true&db=eric&AN=ED025688&site=ehost-live.

Tracy, Brian. "5 Ways to Gain a Competitive Advantage: The Importance of Continuous Learning and Personal Development." *Brian Tracy's Blog* (blog), October 11, 2012. http://www.briantracy.com/blog/personal-success/5-ways-to-gain-a-competitive-advantage-the-importance-of-continuous-learning-and-personal-development/.

Tran, Mark. "The Secret Literary Life of George W Bush." *The Guardian*, December 30, 2008, sec. US news. https://www.theguardian.com/world/deadlineusa/2008/dec/30/georgebush-usa.

Troy, Tevi. "8 Fascinating Stories about Presidents and Their Favorite Books." Business Insider, February 17, 2014. http://www.businessinsider.com/8-surprising-tales-of-presidential-reading-2014-2.

VanBuren, Emily. "7 Apps for Cataloguing Your Home Library." Inside HigherEd, June 12, 2014. https://www.insidehighered.com/blogs/gradhacker/7-apps-cataloguing-your-home-library#sthash.XJwyHHQF.Tuj4REbV.dpbs.

Vital, Anna. "How Elon Musk Started - His Life Visualized." *Funders and Founders* (blog), February 23, 2016. http://fundersandfounders.com/how-elon-musk-started/.

Vozza, Stephanie. "Why You Should Read 50 Books This Year (and How to Do It)." Fast Company, January 21, 2016. http://www.fastcompany.com/3055608/work-smart/why-you-should-read-50-books-this-year-and-how-to-do-it.

Webb, Bert. "Twelve Ways to Mark up a Book." Open Loops, February 20, 2006. http://hwebbjr.typepad.com/openloops/2006/02/twelve_ways_to_.html.

Weissmann, Jordan. "The Decline of the American Book Lover." *The Atlantic*, January 21, 2014. http://www.theatlantic.com/business/archive/2014/01/the-decline-of-the-american-book-lover/283222/.

Weller, Martin. *The Digital Scholar: How Technology Is Transforming Scholarly Practice*. London: Bloomsbury, 2011.

White, Caitlin. "U.S. Independent Bookstores Thriving, despite Major Declines across the Pond." Bustle, February 26, 2015. http://www.bustle.com/articles/66629-us-independent-bookstores-thriving-despite-major-declines-across-the-pond.

Williams, Ray. "The Cult of Ignorance in the United States: Anti-Intellectualism and the 'Dumbing down' of America." SOTT.net, June 7, 2014. https://www.sott.net/article/313177-The-cult-of-ignorance-in-the-United-States-Anti-intellectualism-and-the-dumbing-down-of-America.

Willingham, Daniel. "Is Listening to an Audio Book 'Cheating?'" Daniel Willingham--Science & Education, July 24, 2016. http://www.danielwillingham.com/1/post/2016/07/is-listening-to-an-audio-book-cheating.html.

Wilson, Douglas. "Honor's Voice." The New Yorks Times, 1998. http://www.nytimes.com/books/first/w/wilson-voice.html.

Winter-Hébert, Lana. "10 Benefits of Reading: Why You Should Read Every Day." Lifehack. Accessed June 26, 2016. http://www.lifehack.org/articles/lifestyle/10-benefits-reading-why-you-should-read-everyday.html.

Winters, Dick, and Cole Kingseed. *Beyond Band of Brothers*. LRG edition. Waterville, Me.: Large Print Press, 2008.

Wise, Abigail. "8 Science-Backed Reasons to Read a (Real) Book." Real Simple. Accessed July 22, 2016. http://www.realsimple.com/health/preventative-health/benefits-of-reading-real-books.

Womack, Sid T., and B. J. Chandler. "Encouraging Reading for Professional Development." *Journal of Reading* 35, no. 5 (February 1992): 390.

Wong, JJ. "8 Reasons Why Reading Is so Important." *Inspiration Boost* (blog), 2012. http://www.inspirationboost.com/8-reasons-why-reading-is-so-important.

Wu, Gary. "How Reading Impacted Warren Buffett, Mark Cuban, and Malcolm X." Gary Wu, October 16, 2014. http://www.garywu.net/influential-people-importance-reading/.

Young, Scott. "I Was Wrong about Speed Reading: Here Are the Facts." Scott H. Young, January 2015. https://www.scotthyoung.com/blog/2015/01/19/speed-reading-redo/.

Zakaria, Fareed. *In Defense of a Liberal Education*, 2016.

Zetlin, Minda. "8 Highly Effective Habits That Helped Make Bill Gates the Richest Man on Earth." Inc.com, May 3, 2016. http://www.inc.com/minda-zetlin/8-highly-effective-habits-that-helped-make-bill-gates-the-richest-man-on-earth.html.

Zickuhr, Kathryn, and Maeve Duggan. "E-Book Reading Jumps; Print Book Reading Declines." Washington, D.C.: Pew Research Center, December 27, 2012. http://libraries.pewinternet.org/files/legacy-pdf/PIP_Reading%20and%20ebooks_12.27.pdf.

Zickuhr, Kathryn, Kristen Purcell, and Lee Rainie. "From Distance Admirers to Library Lovers-and Beyond." Washington, D.C.: Pew Research Center, March 2014. http://www.pewinternet.org/files/2014/03/PIP-Library-Typology-Report_031314.pdf.

Zickuhr, Kathryn, and Lee Rainie. "E-Reading Rises as Device Ownership Jumps." Washington, D.C.: Pew Research Center, January 2014. http://www.pewinternet.org/files/2014/01/PIP_E-reading_011614.pdf.

Endnotes

1. Erin Dooley, "Here's Obama's Childhood Reading List," *ABC News*, May 1, 2015, http://abcnews.go.com/Politics/president-obama-childhood-reading-list/story?id=30703821.
2. Stan Skrabut, "A Study of Informal Learning Among University of Wyoming Extension Educators" (University of Wyoming, 2013).
3. Ibid., 98.
4. Ibid., 6.
5. Donald Hernandez, "Double Jeopardy: How Third-Grade Reading Skills and Poverty Influence High School Graduation" (University at Albany, State University of New York: The Annie E. Casey Foundation, April 2011), https://www.fcd-us.org/assets/2016/04/DoubleJeopardyReport.pdf; "Third-Grade Reading Legislation," NCSL: National Conference of State Legislatures, May 23, 2018, http://www.ncsl.org/research/education/third-grade-reading-legislation.aspx.
6. Martin Weller, *The Digital Scholar: How Technology Is Transforming Scholarly Practice* (London: Bloomsbury, 2011).
7. Ralph M. Besse, "The Philosophy of Reading," *Foundation for Economic Education*, January 1, 1956, https://fee.org/articles/the-philosophy-of-reading/.
8. Ibid., para. 39.
9. David Cottrell, *Tuesday Morning Coaching: Eight Simple Truths to Boost Your Career and Your Life* (New York: McGraw-Hill, 2013).
10. Natasha Postolovski, "The Transformative Effects of Reading + Elon Musk's Reading List," *Inside Envato*, January 21, 2015, http://inside.envato.com/the-transformative-effects-of-reading-elon-musks-reading-list/.
11. Andrew Perrin, "Who Doesn't Read Books in America?," *Pew Research Center* (blog), March 23, 2018, http://www.pewresearch.org/fact-tank/2018/03/23/who-doesnt-read-books-in-america/.
12. Kathryn Zickuhr and Lee Rainie, "E-Reading Rises as Device Ownership Jumps" (Washington, D.C.: Pew Research Center, January 2014), http://www.pewinternet.org/files/2014/01/PIP_E-reading_011614.pdf.
13. Jordan Weissmann, "The Decline of the American Book Lover," *The Atlantic*, January 21, 2014, http://www.theatlantic.com/business/archive/2014/01/the-decline-of-the-american-book-lover/283222/.
14. Zickuhr and Rainie, "E-Reading Rises as Device Ownership Jumps"; Weissmann, "The Decline of the American Book Lover."
15. "Millennials Want to Make Books Cool Again," *Fortune* (blog), June 7, 2016, http://fortune.com/2016/06/07/millennials-physical-books/.
16. Zickuhr and Rainie, "E-Reading Rises as Device Ownership Jumps."
17. Ibid.
18. Sara Kehaulani Goo, "The Skills Americans Say Kids Need to Succeed in Life,"

Pew Research Center, February 19, 2015, http://www.pewresearch.org/fact-tank/2015/02/19/skills-for-success/.

19. Lee Rainie et al., "The Rise of E-Reading," *Pew Internet Libraries*, 2012, http://libraries.pewinternet.org/2012/04/04/the-rise-of-e-reading/.

20. Ibid.

21. Thomas C. Corley, "Reading Habits of the Affluent," *Rich Habits Institute*, May 13, 2014, http://richhabits.net/reading-habits-of-the-rich-what-the-wealthy-read/.

22. Carolyn Miller, Kristen Purcell, and Lee Rainie, "Reading Habits in Different Communities" (Washington, D.C.: Pew Research Center's Internet & American Life Project, December 20, 2012), http://libraries.pewinternet.org/files/legacy-pdf/LibrariesAndReading_CommunityTypes_12.20.12.pdf.

23. Zickuhr and Rainie, "E-Reading Rises as Device Ownership Jumps."

24. Miller, Purcell, and Rainie, "Reading Habits in Different Communities."

25. Weissmann, "The Decline of the American Book Lover."

26. Kathleen Elkins, "A Self-Made Millionaire Who Studied 1,200 Wealthy People Found They All Have One—Free—Pastime in Common," August 21, 2015, http://www.businessinsider.com/rich-people-like-to-read-2015-8.

27. J. Gilbert and B. Fister, "Reading, Risk, and Reality: College Students and Reading for Pleasure," *College & Research Libraries* 72, no. 5 (September 1, 2011): 474–95, doi:10.5860/crl-148.

28. Cited in Ray Williams, "The Cult of Ignorance in the United States: Anti-Intellectualism and the 'Dumbing Down' of America," *SOTT.net*, June 7, 2014, https://www.sott.net/article/313177-The-cult-of-ignorance-in-the-United-States-Anti-intellectualism-and-the-dumbing-down-of-America.

29. Cited in Jackie Greene and Linda Serro, "Encouraging Critical Thinking and Professional Reading with Literacy Bags," *The Open Communication Journal* 9, no. Supp11: M10 (2015): 65–71; Valerie Strauss, "Most Literate Nation in the World? Not the U.S., New Ranking Says.," *Washington Post*, March 8, 2016, https://www.washingtonpost.com/news/answer-sheet/wp/2016/03/08/most-literate-nation-in-the-world-not-the-u-s-new-ranking-says/.

30. Lydia Burak, "Examining and Predicting College Students' Reading Intentions and Behaviors: An Application of the Theory of Reasoned Action," *Reading Horizon* 45, no. 2 (December 2004): 139–53; SuHua Huang et al., "Reading Habits of College Students in the United States," *Reading Psychology* 35, no. 5 (July 4, 2014): 437–67, doi:10.1080/02702711.2012.739593.

31. Anthony J. Applegate et al., "The Peter Effect Revisited: Reading Habits and Attitudes of College Students," *Literacy Research and Instruction* 53, no. 3 (July 3, 2014): 189, doi:10.1080/19388071.2014.898719.

32. Cited in Molly Redden, "7 in 10 Students Have Skipped Buying a Textbook because of Its Cost," *The Chronicle of Higher Education*, August 23, 2011, http://www.chronicle.com/article/7-in-10-Students-Have-Skipped/128785/.

33. Nancy M. Foasberg, "Adoption of E-book Readers among College Students: A

Survey," *Information Technology and Libraries* 30, no. 3 (September 2, 2011), http://ejournals.bc.edu/ojs/index.php/ital/article/view/1769.

34. Ibid.

35. Rebecca Alber, "5 Reasons to Read for Reluctant Readers," *Edutopia*, April 28, 2016, http://www.edutopia.org/blog/5-reading-reasons-reluctant-readers-rebecca-alber.

36. Applegate et al., "The Peter Effect Revisited."

37. Gilbert and Fister, "Reading, Risk, and Reality."

38. Applegate et al., "The Peter Effect Revisited."

39. Ibid., 193.

40. Jonathan Douglas, "The Importance of Instilling a Need to Read," *The Telegraph*, May 4, 2013, sec. Education, http://www.telegraph.co.uk/education/educationopinion/10035473/The-importance-of-instilling-a-need-to-read.html.

41. Applegate et al., "The Peter Effect Revisited."

42. Gilbert and Fister, "Reading, Risk, and Reality"; Applegate et al., "The Peter Effect Revisited"; Huang et al., "Reading Habits of College Students in the United States."

43. Huang et al., "Reading Habits of College Students in the United States."

44. Ibid.

45. Ashley Thorne, "Students Will Rise When Colleges Challenge Them to Read Good Books," The Chronicle of Higher Education, March 13, 2016, http://chronicle.com/article/Students-Will-Rise-When/235681/, para. 8.

46. Foasberg, "Adoption of E-book Readers Among College Students."

47. Gilbert and Fister, "Reading, Risk, and Reality".

48. Ibid., 490.

49. Kevin Kelly, *The Inevitable: Understanding the 12 Technological Forces That Will Shape Our Future* (New York, New York: Viking, 2016), 168.

50. Michael Hyatt, "5 Ways Reading Makes You a Better Leader," *Michael Hyatt*, May 4, 2015, http://michaelhyatt.com/science-readers-leaders.html.

51. Stephanie Vozza, "Why You Should Read 50 Books This Year (and How to Do It)," *Fast Company*, January 21, 2016, http://www.fastcompany.com/3055608/work-smart/why-you-should-read-50-books-this-year-and-how-to-do-it.

52. Corley, "Reading Habits of the Affluent."

53. Postolovski, "The Transformative Effects of Reading + Elon Musk's Reading List."

54. Kevin Curry, "Learn from the Reading Habits of Successful People," *ZipRage*, April 20, 2016, https://ziprage.com/learn-from-the-reading-habits-of-successful-people/.

55. Postolovski, "The Transformative Effects of Reading + Elon Musk's Reading List."

56. Thomas C. Corley, "Reading and Success—a Simple Matter of Cause and Effect," *Rich Habits Institute*, April 17, 2014, http://richhabits.net/is-there-a-correlation-between-being-rich-and-reading-habits/; Curry, "Learn from the

Reading Habits of Successful People."

57. Andrew Merle, "The Reading Habits of Ultra-Successful People," *The Huffington Post*, April 16, 2016, para. 9, http://www.huffingtonpost.com/andrew-merle/the-reading-habits-of-ult_b_9688130.html.

58. While I listened to this podcast episode, *Entrepreneurs on Fire* does not list this specific episode on its site.

59. Michael Simmons, "9 Creative Ways to Find Books That Will Make You a Genius," *Forbes*, September 24, 2015, http://www.forbes.com/sites/michaelsimmons/2015/09/24/9-creative-ways-to-find-books-that-will-make-you-a-genius/#15d7db892c47.

60. Jonathan M. Acuff, *Start: Punch Fear in the Face, Escape Average, Do Work That Matters* (Brentwood, Tennessee: Lampo Press, 2013).

61. Libby Kane, "What Rich People Have Next to Their Beds," *Business Insider*, June 17, 2014, http://www.businessinsider.com/rich-people-read-self-improvement-books-2014-6.

62. Shane Parrish, "Jeff Bezos's Reading List," The Week, October 22, 2013, http://theweek.com/articles/458345/jeff-bezoss-reading-list.

63. Fareed Zakaria, *In Defense of a Liberal Education*, 2016.

64. Brian Tracy, "5 Ways to Gain a Competitive Advantage: The Importance of Continuous Learning and Personal Development," *Brian Tracy's Blog* (blog), October 11, 2012, http://www.briantracy.com/blog/personal-success/5-ways-to-gain-a-competitive-advantage-the-importance-of-continuous-learning-and-personal-development/.

65. Rebecca Staton-Reinstein, "Why Successful Business Leaders Love History," *ReliablePlant*, accessed November 13, 2016, http://reliableplant.com/Read/13569/why-successful-business-leaders-love-history.

66. Tim Patrick, "Keeping Up with the Jeffersons," *Well-Read Man*, July 14, 2011, http://wellreadman.comb/2011/07/14/keeping-up-with-jefferson/.

67. Martin Cothran, "The Classical Education of the Founding Fathers," *Memoria Press*, April 15, 2007, https://www.memoriapress.com/articles/classical-education-founding-fathers/.

68. Ibid. para. 7.

69. Ibid. para. 26.

70. Tevi Troy, "8 Fascinating Stories about Presidents and Their Favorite Books," *Business Insider*, February 17, 2014, http://www.businessinsider.com/8-surprising-tales-of-presidential-reading-2014-2.

71. Endrina Tay, "Jefferson, Thomas and Books," *Encyclopedia Virginia*, November 21, 2016, http://www.encyclopediavirginia.org/Jefferson_Thomas_and_Books. Para. 3.

72. Ibid., Library Organization, para. 5.

73. Ibid., para. 1.

74. Ibid.

75. The Literacy Company, "Some Well-Known Speed Readers," *The Literacy*

Company, 2016, http://www.readfaster.com/articles/well-known-speed-readers.asp.

76. Taylor Pipes, "Taking Note: What Commonplace Books Can Teach Us about Our Past," *Evernote Blog*, February 26, 2016, https://blog.evernote.com/blog/2016/02/26/taking-note-what-commonplace-books-can-teach-us-about-our-past/.

77. Tay, "Jefferson, Thomas and Books."

78. Ibid.

79. Ibid.

80. Benjamin Franklin and E. Boyd (Elmer Boyd) Smith, *Autobiography of Benjamin Franklin*, ed. Frank Woodworth Pine, 2006, http://www.gutenberg.org/e-books/20203.

81. Ibid.

82. Ibid.

83. Ibid.

84. Ibid., VII—Beginning Business in Philadelphia, para. 20.

85. Ibid.

86. Ibid., VIII—Business Success and First Public Service, para. 21.

87. Empact, "Why Constant Learners All Embrace the 5-Hour Rule," *Inc.com*, June 20, 2016, http://www.inc.com/empact/why-constant-learners-all-embrace-the-5-hour-rule.html.

88. "Letter from John Adams to Abigail Adams, Post 12 May 1780," accessed November 11, 2016, https://www.masshist.org/digitaladams/archive/doc?id=L17800512jasecond.

89. Beth Prindle, ed., "John Adams Unbound" (American Library Association, 2008), http://www.ala.org/programming/sites/ala.org.programming/files/content/adams/files/34%2520Exhibit%2520script.doc.

90. Katherine Manning, "John Adams and His Classical Heritage," accessed November 15, 2016, http://college.holycross.edu/faculty/wziobro/ClassicalAmerica/johnadams.htm.

91. Ibid.

92. Ibid., para. 3.

93. Prindle, "John Adams Unbound."

94. Manning, "John Adams and His Classical Heritage."

95. Prindle, "John Adams Unbound."

96. Ibid., The Library, para. 1

97. Ibid., A Family Affair, para. 4.

98. Ibid.

99. William Chrystal, "What Is a Good Citizen? Thoughts from Some of the Founding Fathers," *The Federalist Papers*, May 18, 2013, http://thefederalistpapers.org/current-events/what-is-a-good-citizen-thoughts-from-some-of-the-founding-fathers.

100. Cited in Ibid., para. 2.

101. "The Best-Read Presidents," *The Daily Beast*, February 14, 2010, http://www.thedailybeast.com/galleries/2010/02/14/the-best-read-presidents.html.

102. Shane Parrish, "George Washington's Practical Self-Education," *Farnam Street*, June 13, 2016, https://www.farnamstreetblog.com/2016/06/george-washington-self-education/.

103. American Antiquarian Society, "Personal Libraries: Washington," *A Place of Reading*, 2010, http://www.americanantiquarian.org/Exhibitions/Reading/washington.htm.

104. Parrish, "George Washington's Practical Self-Education." para. 5.

105. The Literacy Company, "Some Well-Known Speed Readers."

106. Parrish, "George Washington's Practical Self-Education," *Studying for Success*, para. 6.

107. American Antiquarian Society, "Personal Libraries: Washington"; Bruce, "Career Hacks from Young George Washington," *Project Management Hacks*, March 10, 2015, http://projectmanagementhacks.com/career-hacks-young-george-washington/.

108. "The Best-Read Presidents."

109. American Antiquarian Society, "Personal Libraries: Washington."

110. Harold Evans, "White House Book Club," *The New York Times*, January 14, 2001, http://www.nytimes.com/books/01/01/14/bookend/bookend.html.

111. Troy, "8 Fascinating Stories about Presidents and Their Favorite Books."

112. Ibid.

113. Ibid.

114. Ibid.

115. Michael D. Shear, "Obama after Dark: The Precious Hours Alone," *The New York Times*, July 2, 2016, http://www.nytimes.com/2016/07/03/us/politics/obama-after-dark-the-precious-hours-alone.html.

116. Michael Medved, "Obama's Revealing Book Bag," *The Daily Beast*, August 23, 2011, http://www.thedailybeast.com/articles/2011/08/23/obama-s-fictional-world-a-peek-at-his-vacation-reading-list.html; Jessica Stillman, "Mark Zuckerberg and President Obama Both Read Fiction (You Should Too)," *Inc.com*, November 2, 2015, http://www.inc.com/jessica-stillman/why-mark-zuckerberg-likes-to-kick-back-with-a-page-turner-and-why-you-should-too.html.

117. Alison Flood, "President Obama Says Novels Taught Him 'the Most Important' Things about Being a Citizen," *RawStory*, October 28, 2015, http://www.rawstory.com/2015/10/president-obama-says-novels-taught-him-the-most-important-things-about-being-a-citizen/; Thu-Huong Ha, "Barack Obama Says He Learned How to Be a Good Citizen from Reading Novels," *Quartz*, October 27, 2015, http://qz.com/534165/barack-obama-says-he-learned-how-to-be-a-good-citizen-from-reading-novels/.

118. Flood, "President Obama Says Novels Taught Him 'the Most Important' Things about Being a Citizen."

119. Troy, "8 Fascinating Stories about Presidents and Their Favorite Books."

120. Tracy Mumford, "A Bookish Tour through Obama's Years in the White House," January 19, 2017, http://www.mprnews.org/story/2017/01/19/books-obama-years-book-tour.

121. Troy, "8 Fascinating Stories about Presidents and Their Favorite Books," para. 23.

122. Karl Rove, "Bush Is a Book Lover," *Wall Street Journal*, December 26, 2008, sec. Opinion, http://www.wsj.com/articles/SB123025595706634689.

123. Mark Tran, "The Secret Literary Life of George W Bush," *The Guardian*, December 30, 2008, sec. US news, https://www.theguardian.com/world/deadlineusa/2008/dec/30/georgebush-usa.

124. Rove, "Bush Is a Book Lover," para. 16.

125. Troy, "8 Fascinating Stories about Presidents and Their Favorite Books."

126. Walt Harrington, "Dubya and Me," *The American Scholar*, August 25, 2011, https://theamericanscholar.org/dubya-and-me/#.

127. Rove, "Bush Is a Book Lover"; Tran, "The Secret Literary Life of George W Bush"; Troy, "8 Fascinating Stories about Presidents and Their Favorite Books."

128. Harrington, "Dubya and Me."

129. Troy, "8 Fascinating Stories about Presidents and Their Favorite Books."

130. Harrington, "Dubya and Me," para. 81.

131. Troy, "8 Fascinating Stories about Presidents and Their Favorite Books."

132. "The Best-Read Presidents."

133. William H. Honan, "Books, Books and More Books: Clinton an Omnivorous Reader," *The New York Times*, December 10, 1992, sec. Books, http://www.nytimes.com/1992/12/10/books/books-books-and-more-books-clinton-an-omnivorous-reader.html.

134. Jaime Fuller, "BREAKING: President Obama Hates Cable News," *Washington Post*, September 26, 2014, https://www.washingtonpost.com/news/the-fix/wp/2014/09/26/breaking-president-obama-hates-cable-news/; Honan, "Books, Books and More Books."

135. Honan, "Books, Books and More Books."

136. Ibid.

137. Fuller, "BREAKING."

138. Honan, "Books, Books and More Books."

139. Troy, "8 Fascinating Stories about Presidents and Their Favorite Books."

140. Kendra Kinnison, "How John F. Kennedy Used Discipline and Creativity to Become President," *Coach Kendra*, August 3, 2012, http://kendrakinnison.com/john-f-kennedy/.

141. Ibid.

142. John F. Kennedy biography, "John F. Kennedy Biography—Life, Family, Childhood, Children, Death, History, Wife, School, Mother," *Encyclopedia of World Biographies*, accessed November 12, 2016, http://www.notablebiographies.com/Jo-Ki/Kennedy-John-F.html.

143. Peter Grier, "John F. Kennedy: Why Books Were a Big Part of His Life," *Chris-*

tian Science Monitor, November 23, 2013, http://www.csmonitor.com/USA/Politics/Decoder/2013/1123/John-F.-Kennedy-Why-books-were-a-big-part-of-his-life-video.

144. The Lieutenant, "5 Life Lessons from JFK," *Return of the Kings* (blog), December 6, 2013, http://www.returnofkings.com/22635/5-life-lessons-from-jfk.

145. The Literacy Company, "Some Well-Known Speed Readers."

146. Ibid.

147. The Lieutenant, "5 Life Lessons from JFK."

148. Kinnison, "How John F. Kennedy Used Discipline and Creativity to Become President."

149. Cited in Fuller, "BREAKING."

150. "The Best-Read Presidents."

151. Evans, "White House Book Club"; "The Best-Read Presidents."

152. "Franklin D. Roosevelt," Wikipedia, December 23, 2017, https://en.wikipedia.org/w/index.php?title=Franklin_D._Roosevelt&oldid=816761211.

153. The Literacy Company, "Some Well-Known Speed Readers."

154. Ibid.

155. Ibid.

156. Evans, "White House Book Club."

157. "The Best-Read Presidents"; Troy, "8 Fascinating Stories about Presidents and Their Favorite Books."

158. Karl Smallwood, "Theodore Roosevelt Could Read a Book before Breakfast," *Fact Fiend*, July 15, 2014, http://www.factfiend.com/theodore-roosevelt-read-book-breakfast/.

159. Alex Birkett, "Think Like a Rough Rider: Productivity Hacks from Teddy Roosevelt," *The Roosevelts*, September 22, 2014, http://www.rsvlts.com/2014/09/22/productivity-hacks-from-teddy-roosevelt/; Brett McKay, "How to Speed Read Like Theodore Roosevelt," *The Art of Manliness*, October 18, 2009, http://www.artofmanliness.com/2009/10/18/how-to-speed-read-like-theodore-roosevelt/.

160. Jeremy Anderberg, "Theodore Roosevelt's Reading List," *The Art of Manliness*, February 3, 2014, http://www.artofmanliness.com/2014/02/03/the-libraries-of-great-men-theodore-roosevelts-reading-list/; Smallwood, "Theodore Roosevelt Could Read a Book before Breakfast."

161. Troy, "8 Fascinating Stories about Presidents and Their Favorite Books."

162. Robert Talbert, "Teddy Roosevelt's to-Do List," *Casting Out Nines*, August 18, 2008, https://castingoutnines.wordpress.com/2008/08/18/teddy-roosevelts-to-do-list/.

163. Troy, "8 Fascinating Stories about Presidents and Their Favorite Books."

164. The Literacy Company, "Some Well-Known Speed Readers"; Douglas Wilson, "Honor's Voice," *The New York Times*, 1998, http://www.nytimes.com/books/first/w/wilson-voice.html.

165. Wilson, "Honor's Voice."

166. Kris Heap, "The 8 Amazing Habits of Abraham Lincoln," *Successify!*, March 28, 2013, http://successify.net/2013/03/28/the-8-amazing-habits-of-abraham-lincoln/.

167. Evans, "White House Book Club"; Heap, "The 8 Amazing Habits of Abraham Lincoln"; Judy Lin, "10 Questions for Abraham Lincoln Scholar Ronald C. White Jr.," *UCLA Newsroom*, February 12, 2009, http://newsroom.ucla.edu/stories/10-questions-for-abraham-lincoln-81493; Wilson, "Honor's Voice."

168. Kenneth J. Winkle, "Abraham Lincoln: Self-Made Man," *Journal of the Abraham Lincoln Association* 21, no. 2 (Summer 2000), http://hdl.handle.net/2027/spo.2629860.0021.203.

169. AoM Team, "Books That Influenced Abraham Lincoln," *The Art of Manliness*, September 15, 2015, http://www.artofmanliness.com/2015/09/15/the-libraries-of-famous-men-abraham-lincoln/.

170. Wilson, "Honor's Voice."

171. Ibid., para. 4.

172. Jon Birdsong, "5 Learnings from Abraham Lincoln before He Turned 40," *WideAngle*, August 7, 2016, https://wideangle.com/blog/2016/08/learning-abraham-lincoln.

173. AoM Team, "Books That Influenced Abraham Lincoln."

174. Cited in Birdsong, "5 Learnings from Abraham Lincoln before He Turned 40," para. 14

175. Troy, "8 Fascinating Stories about Presidents and Their Favorite Books."

176. AoM Team, "Books That Influenced Abraham Lincoln."

177. The Literacy Company, "Some Well-Known Speed Readers." Abraham Lincoln.

178. Crispin Burke, "6 Smart Habits of the US Military's Most Successful Commanders," *Task & Purpose*, April 17, 2015, http://taskandpurpose.com/6-smart-habits-of-the-us-militarys-most-successful-commanders.

179. Ibid.

180. Parrish, "George Washington's Practical Self-Education."

181. Joe Byerly, "Use 'mental Models' to Outthink the Enemy," *Association of the United States Army*, August 15, 2016, https://www.ausa.org/articles/use-%E2%80%98mental-models%E2%80%99-outthink-enemy.

182. Cited in Geoffrey Ingersoll, "General James 'Mad Dog' Mattis Email about Being 'Too Busy to Read' Is a Must-Read," *Business Insider*, May 9, 2013, http://www.businessinsider.com/viral-james-mattis-email-reading-marines-2013-5. para. 10.

183. Ibid., para. 7–8.

184. Seth Mandel, "The Silly Plan to Draft Gen. Mattis Shows What's Wrong with GOP," *New York Post*, April 26, 2016, http://nypost.com/2016/04/25/the-silly-plan-to-draft-gen-mattis-shows-whats-wrong-with-gop/.

185. "George Patton," *DyslexiaHelp*, 2016, http://dyslexiahelp.umich.edu/success-stories/george-patton.

186. Encyclopedia.com, "Patton, George S.—Dictionary Definition of Patton, George S. | Encyclopedia.com: FREE Online Dictionary," accessed October 29, 2016, http://www.encyclopedia.com/history/educational-magazines/patton-george-s.

187. Ibid.

188. Ibid.

189. Ibid.

190. J. Furman Daniel III, "Patton as a Counterinsurgent?: Lessons from an Unlikely COIN-Danista," *Small Wars Journal*, January 25, 2014, http://smallwarsjournal.com/jrnl/art/patton-as-a-counterinsurgent-lessons-from-an-unlikely-coin-danista.

191. Byerly, "Use 'Mental Models' to Outthink the Enemy."

192. Jeffrey Sanderson, "General George S. Patton Jr.: Master of Operational Battle Command. What Lasting Battle Command Lessons Can We Learn from Him?" (School of Advanced Military Studies, United States Army Command and General Staff College, May 22, 1997), http://www.dtic.mil/dtic/tr/fulltext/u2/a331356.pdf.

193. Daniel III, "Patton as a Counterinsurgent?: Lessons from an Unlikely COIN-Danista."

194. Ibid., para. 30.

195. Jeffrey Sanderson, "General George S. Patton Jr.: Master of Operational Battle Command. What Lasting Battle Command Lessons Can We Learn from Him?" (May 22, 1997), http://www.dtic.mil/dtic/tr/fulltext/u2/a331356.pdf.

196. Ibid., p. 27.

197. Byerly, "Use 'Mental Models' to Outthink the Enemy."

198. Ibid.

199. Cited in Ibid., para. 11.

200. Cited in Brett McKay, "George Patton Letter to His Son," *The Art of Manliness*, August 21, 2011, http://www.artofmanliness.com/2011/08/21/manvotional-a-letter-from-general-george-s-patton-to-his-son/.

201. Byerly, "Use 'Mental Models' to Outthink the Enemy."

202. Alexander Lovelace, "Patton's Last Command," *Warfare History Network*, September 13, 2016, http://warfarehistorynetwork.com/daily/wwii/pattons-last-command/.

203. Ibid., para. 8.

204. Tim Ferriss, "General Stan McChrystal on Eating One Meal per Day, Special Ops, and Mental Toughness," *The Tim Ferriss Show*, July 5, 2015, http://fourhourworkweek.com/2015/07/05/stanley-mcchrystal/.

205. General Stanley McChrystal, *My Share of the Task: A Memoir*, reprint edition (Portfolio Trade, 2014).

206. Ferriss, "General Stan McChrystal on Eating One Meal per Day, Special Ops, and Mental Toughness."

207. Timothy Ferriss, *Tools of Titans: The Tactics, Routines, and Habits of Billion-*

aires, Icons, and World-Class Performers (Boston: Houghton Mifflin Harcourt, 2016).

208. Stan McChrystal, "How I Keep Up with an Unrelenting Work Pace," *LinkedIn Pulse*, February 1, 2016, https://www.linkedin.com/pulse/my-life-outside-work-how-i-keep-up-unrelenting-pace-stan-mcchrystal.

209. Ferriss, "General Stan McChrystal on Eating One Meal per Day, Special Ops, and Mental Toughness."

210. Dan Schawbel, "General Stanley McChrystal: Leadership Lessons from Afghanistan," *Forbes*, January 10, 2013, http://www.forbes.com/sites/danschawbel/2013/01/10/general-stanley-mcchrystal-leadership-lessons-from-afghanistan/.

211. McChrystal, "How I Keep Up with an Unrelenting Work Pace."

212. Dick Winters and Cole Kingseed, *Beyond Band of Brothers*, LRG edition (Waterville, ME: Large Print Press, 2008), pp. 285–286.

213. Staton-Reinstein, "Why Successful Business Leaders Love History."

214. Donald Latumahina, "How Business Leaders Read," *Life Optimizer*, January 26, 2008, http://www.lifeoptimizer.org/2008/01/25/reading-tips-how-business-leaders-read/.

215. Elkins, "A Self-Made Millionaire Who Studied 1,200 Wealthy People Found They All Have One — Free — Pastime in Common."

216. John Coleman, "For Those Who Want to Lead, Read," *Harvard Business Review*, August 15, 2012, https://hbr.org/2012/08/for-those-who-want-to-lead-rea, para. 3.

217. Latumahina, "How Business Leaders Read"; Harriet Rubin, "C.E.O. Libraries Reveal Keys to Success," *The New York Times*, July 21, 2007, http://www.nytimes.com/2007/07/21/business/21libraries.html.

218. Elkins, "A Self-Made Millionaire Who Studied 1,200 Wealthy People Found They All Have One—Free—Pastime in Common."

219. Rubin, "C.E.O. Libraries Reveal Keys to Success," para. 3.

220. Minda Zetlin, "8 Highly Effective Habits That Helped Make Bill Gates the Richest Man on Earth," *Inc.com*, May 3, 2016, http://www.inc.com/minda-zetlin/8-highly-effective-habits-that-helped-make-bill-gates-the-richest-man-on-earth.html.

221. Ben Austin, "'Billionaire' Reading Habits: 11 Ways to Read 52 Books in 52 Weeks, 2X Your Reading Speed and Improve Your Comprehension by 500%," *Stop. Start. Do.*, accessed November 15, 2016, http://www.stopstartdo.com/blog/become-billionaire-smart-how-to-read-52-books-in-52-weeks.

222. Mark Morgan Ford, "An Idea for You from Bill Gates That Will Help You Take a Giant Step Forward," *Early to Rise*, April 4, 2005, http://www.earlytorise.com/an-idea-for-you-from-bill-gates-that-will-help-you-take-a-giant-step-forward/.

223. Jonathon Sturgeon, "Reading Habits of the Rich and Powerful, 2016 Edition: Gates, Zuckerberg, Obama," *Flavorwire*, January 7, 2016, http://

flavorwire.com/554696/reading-habits-of-the-rich-and-powerful-2016-edition-gates-zuckerberg-obama.

224. Gerald Beals, "Edison Biography," *ThomasEdison.com*, 1999, http://www.thomasedison.com/biography.html.

225. American Chemical Society, "Thomas Edison, Chemist," *American Chemical Society*, 2016, https://www.acs.org/content/acs/en/education/whatischemistry/landmarks/thomas-edison.html.

226. Beals, "Edison Biography"; Biography.com Editors, "Thomas Edison Biography," Biography.com, February 5, 2016, http://www.biography.com/people/thomas-edison-9284349.

227. thepower, "Thomas Edison and His Struggles with Dyslexia," *The Power of Dyslexia*, 2012, http://thepowerofdyslexia.com/thomas-edison/.

228. Beals, "Edison Biography."

229. Ibid.

230. thepower, "Thomas Edison and His Struggles with Dyslexia."

231. Thomas Edison Center, "Thomas Edison and Menlo Park," *Thomas Edison Center at Menlo Park*, 2009, http://www.menloparkmuseum.org/history/thomas-edison-and-menlo-park/. para. 1.

232. Beals, "Edison Biography."

233. American Chemical Society, "Thomas Edison, Chemist."

234. Jim Powell, "The Education of Thomas Edison," *Foundation for Economic Education*, February 1, 1995, https://fee.org/articles/the-education-of-thomas-edison/.

235. Ibid., para. 15.

236. Beals, "Edison Biography."

237. Powell, "The Education of Thomas Edison."

238. Biography.com Editors, "Thomas Edison Biography."

239. "Edisonian Approach," Wikipedia, September 12, 2017, https://en.wikipedia.org/w/index.php?title=Edisonian_approach&oldid=800292477.

240. Sturgeon, "Reading Habits of the Rich and Powerful, 2016 Edition."

241. David Keane, "Read Your Way to Success," *The Art of Deliberate Success*, December 1, 2014, http://artofdeliberatesuccess.com/blog/read-your-way-to-success/.

242. Vozza, "Why You Should Read 50 Books This Year (and How to Do It)."

243. Stillman, "Mark Zuckerberg and President Obama Both Read Fiction (You Should Too)."

244. Anna Vital, "How Elon Musk Started—His Life Visualized," *Funders and Founders*, February 23, 2016, http://fundersandfounders.com/how-elon-musk-started/.

245. Postolovski, "The Transformative Effects of Reading + Elon Musk's Reading List."

246. Vital, "How Elon Musk Started—His Life Visualized."

247. Ibid.

248. Rajiv Mathew, "9 Things to Learn from Elon Musk," *CitizenTekk*, November 21, 2013, http://www.citizentekk.com/elon-musk-qualities/.

249. Linker 2, "Successful People and Their Reading Habits," *Crossroads Staffing Services*, August 5, 2016, http://www.crossroadsstaffing.com/blog/2016_08_05.html; Mathew, "9 Things to Learn from Elon Musk"; Suneel Thomas, "Elon Musk's Secret Sauce to Grow at 10x Speed," *Techachari*, July 9, 2015, http://www.techachari.com/grow-10x-speed/.

250. Postolovski, "The Transformative Effects of Reading + Elon Musk's Reading List"; Vital, "How Elon Musk Started—His Life Visualized."

251. Vital, "How Elon Musk Started—His Life Visualized."

252. Vozza, "Why You Should Read 50 Books This Year (and How to Do It)."

253. John Sviokla and Mitch Cohen, "Mark Cuban Used to Stay Up All Night Reading about Stamps," *Business Insider*, January 7, 2015, http://www.businessinsider.com/mark-cuban-baseball-cards-2015-1.

254. Austin, "'Billionaire' Reading Habits: 11 Ways to Read 52 Books in 52 Weeks, 2X Your Reading Speed and Improve Your Comprehension by 500%."

255. Sheraan Amod, "10 Success Principles from Mark Cuban That Made Him Rich," *Sheraan Amod | Blog*, 2012, http://sheraan.com/post/19865115481/10-success-principles-from-mark-cuban-that-made.

256. Gary Wu, "How Reading Impacted Warren Buffett, Mark Cuban, and Malcolm X," *Gary Wu*, October 16, 2014, http://www.garywu.net/influential-people-importance-reading/.

257. Amod, "10 Success Principles from Mark Cuban That Made Him Rich."

258. Wu, "How Reading Impacted Warren Buffett, Mark Cuban, and Malcolm X."

259. Bruce Harpham, "9 Can't-Miss Secrets behind Warren Buffett's Wealth," *Lifehack*, accessed October 26, 2016, http://www.lifehack.org/articles/money/9-cant-miss-secrets-behind-warren-buffetts-wealth.html; Thomas Oppong, "This Is The Daily Routine of Warren Buffett," July 9, 2014, http://alltopstartups.com/2014/07/09/daily-routine-of-warren-buffett/.

260. Harpham, "9 Can't-Miss Secrets behind Warren Buffett's Wealth."

261. Cited in Wu, "How Reading Impacted Warren Buffett, Mark Cuban, and Malcolm X."

262. Leonard Kniffel, "Reading for Life: Oprah Winfrey," *Ilovelibraries*, August 10, 2011, http://www.ilovelibraries.org/article/reading-life-oprah-winfrey.

263. Ibid., Section: An Angel on Two Continents.

264. Ibid.

265. "Reading Habits: Leaders Are Learners," *Dawn*, June 11, 2011, http://www.dawn.com/2011/06/11/reading-habits-leaders-are-learners/.

266. Gary Stager, "Everything I Know about Reading Instruction I Learned from Oprah Winfrey," *Gary S. Stager*, n.d., http://www.stager.org/articles/oprah.html.

267. Kniffel, "Reading for Life: Oprah Winfrey."

268. Jacqueline Gulledge, "Dolly Parton's Mission to End Illiteracy," *CNN*, November 3, 2016, http://www.cnn.com/2016/11/02/entertainment/iyw-dolly-parton-

imagination-library/index.html.

269. Emerald Pellot, "Dolly Parton's Imagination Library Program Donates Books to Children to Promote Literacy," *LittleThings.com*, accessed November 4, 2016, http://www.littlethings.com/dolly-parton-imagination-library/.

270. Ibid.

271. "Dolly Parton's Imagination Library," 2018, https://imaginationlibrary.com/.

272. Meghashyam Chirravoori, "Why the Reading Habit Is an Amazing Habit to Develop," *Personal-Development-Is-Fun.com*, accessed November 20, 2016, http://www.personal-development-is-fun.com/the-reading-habit.html.

273. Besse, "The Philosophy of Reading."

274. John Coleman, "Why Businesspeople Should Join Book Clubs," Harvard Business Review, February 23, 2016, https://hbr.org/2016/02/why-businesspeople-should-join-book-clubs.

275. Jessica Stillman, "Yet Another Reason You Should Read More: You'll Live Longer," *Inc.com*, August 23, 2016, http://www.inc.com/jessica-stillman/yet-another-reason-you-should-read-more-youll-live-longer.html.

276. Cited in ibid.

277. Heather Levin, "How to Read More Books: Benefits of Reading," *Money Crashers*, October 1, 2012, http://www.moneycrashers.com/read-more-books-benefits/; Glen Stansberry, "Benefits of Reading: 8 Reasons Books Improve Your Life," *LifeDev*, December 17, 2014, http://lifedev.net/2009/06/reading-makes-you-better/.

278. "Benefits of Reading & Advantages of Reading a Book," *Time2Change*, accessed July 17, 2016, https://selfhelpfix.com/benefits-of-reading.php.

279. Stansberry, "Benefits of Reading: 8 Reasons Books Improve Your Life."

280. Lauren Gelman, "Benefits of Reading: Getting Smart, Thin, Healthy, Happy," *Reader's Digest*, September 9, 2013, http://www.rd.com/health/wellness/benefits-of-reading/.

281. Lana Winter-Hébert, "10 Benefits of Reading: Why You Should Read Every Day," *Lifehack*, accessed June 26, 2016, http://www.lifehack.org/articles/lifestyle/10-benefits-reading-why-you-should-read-everyday.html; Gelman, "Benefits of Reading"; Michael Grothaus, "How Changing Your Reading Habits Can Transform Your Health," *Fast Company*, July 27, 2015, http://www.fastcompany.com/3048913/how-to-be-a-success-at-everything/how-changing-your-reading-habits-can-transform-your-health.

282. Abigail Wise, "8 Science-Backed Reasons to Read a (Real) Book," *Real Simple*, accessed July 22, 2016, http://www.realsimple.com/health/preventative-health/benefits-of-reading-real-books.

283. Rachel Grate, "Science Has Great News for People Who Read Actual Books," *Arts.Mic*, September 22, 2014, https://mic.com/articles/99408/science-has-great-news-for-people-who-read-actual-books.

284. Ibid.

285. Gelman, "Benefits of Reading."

286. Wise, "8 Science-Backed Reasons to Read a (Real) Nook."

287. Caroline Myrberg and Ninna Wiberg, "Screen vs. Paper: What Is the Difference for Reading and Learning?," *Insights* 28, no. 2 (July 7, 2015), doi:10.1629/uksg.236.

288. Jason D'Aprile, "In Defense of the E-Reader," *Tech50+* (blog), August 22, 2016, https://tech50plus.com/in-defense-of-the-e-reader/.

289. Grothaus, "How Changing Your Reading Habits Can Transform Your Health."

290. Erin La Rosa, "12 Scientific Ways Reading Can Actually Improve Your Life," *BuzzFeed*, June 7, 2013, http://www.buzzfeed.com/erinlarosa/12-scientific-ways-reading-can-actually-improve-your-life.

291. Gelman, "Benefits of Reading."

292. Shane Parrish, "What You Didn't Know about the Act of Reading Books," *Time*, August 24, 2015, http://time.com/3993897/schopenhauer-reading-books/.

293. Glenn Davis, "Why Is Reading Important?," *Learn to Read*, December 2014, http://www.learn-to-read-prince-george.com/why-is-reading-important.html.

294. Chirravoori, "Why the Reading Habit Is an Amazing Habit to Develop."

295. Shawn Lim, "Why Do You Need to Read Books and the Benefits of It," *Stunning Motivation*, June 23, 2016, http://stunningmotivation.com/why-need-read-books-benefits/.

296. Davis, "Why Is Reading Important?"

297. Levin, "How to Read More Books: Benefits of Reading"; Brad Isaac, "The 26 Major Advantages to Reading More Books and Why 3 in 4 People Are Being Shut out of Success," Persistence Unlimited, December 5, 2007, http://www.persistenceunlimited.com/2007/12/the-26-major-advantages-to-reading-more-books-and-why-3-in-4-people-are-being-shut-out-of-success/.

298. "Benefits of Reading and Advantages of Reading a Book."

299. Davis, "Why Is Reading Important?"

300. Scott McLean, "Learning on the Margins of Adult Education: Self-Help Reading about Health, Relationships, and Career Success," *Studies in the Education of Adults* 46, no. 1 (April 30, 2014): 4–22.

301. Isaac, "The 26 Major Advantages to Reading More Books and Why 3 in 4 People Are Being Shut out of Success."

302. Davis, "Why Is Reading Important?"

303. Justin Miller, "How to Read 52 Books in 52 Weeks and Save Yourself $21,000," *Lifehack*, para. 8, accessed July 23, 2016, http://www.lifehack.org/articles/lifestyle/how-to-read-52-books-in-52-weeks-and-save-yourself-21000.html.

304. Levin, "How to Read More Books: Benefits of Reading"; Winter-Hébert, "10 Benefits of Reading"; JJ Wong, "8 Reasons Why Reading Is so Important," *Inspiration Boost* (blog), 2012, http://www.inspirationboost.com/8-reasons-why-reading-is-so-important; Lim, "Why Do You Need to Read Books and the Bene-

fits of It."

305. McLean, "Learning on the Margins of Adult Education."

306. Brian Tracy, "5 Ways to Gain a Competitive Advantage: The Importance of Continuous Learning and Personal Development," *Brian Tracy's Blog*, October 11, 2012, para., http://www.briantracy.com/blog/personal-success/5-ways-to-gain-a-competitive-advantage-the-importance-of-continuous-learning-and-personal-development/.

307. McLean, "Learning on the Margins of Adult Education," para. 3.

308. Levin, "How to Read More Books: Benefits of Reading," Section: The Benefits of Reading.

309. Stillman, "Mark Zuckerberg and President Obama Both Read Fiction (You Should Too)."; Hyatt, "5 Ways Reading Makes You a Better Leader."

310. George Ambler, "Reading Keeps Leaders Smart, Creative and Social," George Ambler, January 17, 2015, http://www.georgeambler.com/reading-keeps-leaders-smart-creative-social/.

311. Grothaus, "How Changing Your Reading Habits Can Transform Your Health," para. 12.

312. La Rosa, "12 Scientific Ways Reading Can Actually Improve Your Life."

313. Carolyn Martin, "Reading Has Changed in America," *Cornell University New Student Reading Project*, para. 6, accessed July 17, 2016, http://reading.cornell.edu/reading_project_06/gatsby/project.htm.

314. Lim, "Why Do You Need to Read Books and the Benefits of It."

315. Stansberry, "Benefits of Reading: 8 Reasons Books Improve Your Life"; Winter-Hébert, "10 Benefits of Reading"; Gelman, "Benefits of Reading"; Hyatt, "5 Ways Reading Makes You a Better Leader"; La Rosa, "12 Scientific Ways Reading Can Actually Improve Your Life."

316. Gelman, "Benefits of Reading"; La Rosa, "12 Scientific Ways Reading Can Actually Improve Your Life."

317. Stansberry, "Benefits of Reading: 8 Reasons Books Improve Your Life"; Gelman, "Benefits of Reading."; Randall Hansen, "Easy Ways to Improve and Expand Your Vocabulary," EnhanceMyVocabulary.com, accessed October 29, 2016, http://www.enhancemyvocabulary.com/improve-expand-vocabulary.html.

318. Hyatt, "5 Ways Reading Makes You a Better Leader."

319. Wise, "8 Science-Backed Reasons to Read a (Real) Book."; Anne Cunningham and Keith Stanovich, "What Reading Does for the Mind," *American Educator/American Federation of Teachers* Spring/Summer (1998): 1–8.

320. Isaac, "The 26 Major Advantages to Reading More Books and Why 3 in 4 People Are Being Shut Out of Success."

321. Stansberry, "Benefits of Reading: 8 Reasons Books Improve Your Life"; Winter-Hébert, "10 Benefits of Reading."

322. La Rosa, "12 Scientific Ways Reading Can Actually Improve Your Life."

323. Wong, "8 Reasons Why Reading Is So Important."

324. Gelman, "Benefits of Reading"; Isaac, "The 26 Major Advantages to Reading

More Books and Why 3 in 4 People Are Being Shut Out of Success."

325. "Readers Are Leaders: J. N. Whiddon's Tips to Reading 25 Books in a Year," *PRWeb*, March 24, 2016, http://www.prweb.com/releases/2016/03/prweb13266863.htm. para. 7.

326. Srinivas Rao, "How to Read 100 Books in a Year," *The Mission*, October 13, 2016, https://medium.com/the-mission/how-to-read-100-books-in-a-year-d7b35660ebd1#.v4mqicf1u.

327. Laiza King, "6 Practical Tips to Help You Cultivate a Reading Habit," *Huffington Post* (blog), June 6, 2016, http://www.huffingtonpost.com/laiza-king-/6-practical-tips-to-help-_b_10311094.html.

328. Besse, "The Philosophy of Reading."

329. Ibid.

330. Talbert, "Teddy Roosevelt's to-Do List."

331. Rao, "How to Read 100 Books in a Year."

332. Austin, "'Billionaire' Reading Habits: 11 Ways to Read 52 Books in 52 Weeks, 2X Your Reading Speed and Improve Your Comprehension by 500%."

333. "Readers Are Leaders,," para. 4.

334. Shane Parrish, "The Best Way to Find More Time to Read," *Farnam Street*, September 2, 2013, https://www.farnamstreetblog.com/2013/09/finding-time-to-read/.

335. Jeff Goins, "083: How to Build Better Reading Habits and Finish a Book Every Day," Goins, Writer, December 2, 2015, http://goinswriter.com/read-books/.

336. Daniel Willingham, "Is Listening to an Audio Book 'Cheating?,'" Daniel Willingham--Science & Education, July 24, 2016, http://www.danielwillingham.com/1/post/2016/07/is-listening-to-an-audio-book-cheating.html.

337. Isaac, "The 26 Major Advantages to Reading More Books and Why 3 in 4 People Are Being Shut out of Success."

338. Brad Isaac, "5 Sneaky and Underhanded Methods to Add 30% More Time to Your Daily Reading Schedule," Persistence Unlimited, December 14, 2007, http://www.persistenceunlimited.com/2007/12/5-sneaky-and-underhanded-methods-to-add-30-more-time-to-your-daily-reading-schedule/.

339. Parrish, "The Best Way to Find More Time to Read."

340. Ibid.

341. Levin, "How to Read More Books: Benefits of Reading."

342. Betsy Mikel, "How This CEO Finds Time to Read 100 Books a Year," Inc.com, October 19, 2016, http://www.inc.com/betsy-mikel/how-one-ceo-finds-time-to-read-100-books-a-year.html.

343. Besse, "The Philosophy of Reading."

344. Miller, "How to Read 52 Books in 52 Weeks and Save Yourself $21,000." Section How to actually read 52 books in 52 weeks, para. 9.

345. King, "6 Practical Tips to Help You Cultivate a Reading Habit."

346. Anne Bogel, "The 2016 Reading Challenge," *Modern Mrs. Darcy*, December 29,

2015, http://modernmrsdarcy.com/2016-reading-challenge/, para. 2.

347. Johnson O'Connor Research Foundation, "Effective Ways to Build Your Vocabulary," *Johnson O'Connor Research Foundation*, accessed November 1, 2016, http://www.jocrf.org/resources/effective-ways-build-your-vocabulary.

348. Scott Young, "I Was Wrong about Speed Reading: Here Are the Facts," *Scott H. Young*, January 2015, https://www.scotthyoung.com/blog/2015/01/19/speed-reading-redo/.

349. Brett McKay, "How to Build Your Vocabulary in 5 Easy Steps," *The Art of Manliness* (blog), October 3, 2012, http://www.artofmanliness.com/2012/10/03/the-importance-of-building-your-vocabulary-and-5-easy-steps-to-doing-it/.

350. Johnson O'Connor Research Foundation, "Effective Ways to Build Your Vocabulary."

351. McKay, "How to Build Your Vocabulary in 5 Easy Steps."

352. CCC Foundation, "Building a Better Vocabulary," *Capital Community College Foundation*, accessed November 2, 2016, http://grammar.ccc.commnet.edu/grammar/vocabulary.htm.

353. McKay, "How to Build Your Vocabulary in 5 Easy Steps."

354. Ibid.

355. Katherine Hansen, "10 Ways to Build Your Vocabulary," *MyCollegeSuccessStory.com*, accessed October 29, 2016, http://www.mycollegesuccessstory.com/academic-success-tools/build-vocabulary.html. para. 10.

356. Ibid.

357. Johnson O'Connor Research Foundation, "Effective Ways to Build Your Vocabulary."

358. Johnson O'Connor Research Foundation, "Effective Ways to Build Your Vocabulary." Other vocabulary building materials.

359. Ibid.

360. Young, "I Was Wrong about Speed Reading: Here Are the Facts."

361. Tim Ferriss, "Scientific Speed Reading: How to Read 300% Faster in 20 Minutes," *The Time Ferriss Show*, July 30, 2009, http://fourhourworkweek.com/2009/07/30/speed-reading-and-accelerated-learning/.

362. Ibid.

363. The Training Doctor, "Reading Teaches Thinking Skills," *The Training Doctor*, February 26, 2016, http://www.trainingdr.com/reading-teaches-thinking-skills/. para. 7.

364. Thorin Klosowski, "The Truth about Speed Reading," *Lifehacker*, March 13, 2014, http://lifehacker.com/the-truth-about-speed-reading-1542508398.

365. Ibid.

366. Ferriss, "Scientific Speed Reading."

367. "Calculate Your Reading Speed," myReadSpeed.com, 2009, http://www.myreadspeed.com/articles/calculate/.

368. Richard Feldman, "Speed Reading: 10 Tips to Improve Reading Speed and

Comprehension," *Learning Techniques*, 2015, http://www.learningtechniques.com/speedreadingtips.html.

369. Ibid., Prioritize Your Reading

370. Ibid.; McKay, "How to Speed Read Like Theodore Roosevelt"; Young, "I Was Wrong about Speed Reading: Here Are the Facts."

371. Cited in Young, "I Was Wrong about Speed Reading: Here Are the Facts."

372. Feldman, "Speed Reading: 10 Tips to Improve Reading Speed and Comprehension."

373. Young, "I Was Wrong about Speed Reading: Here Are the Facts."

374. Klosowski, "The Truth about Speed Reading."

375. Ferriss, "Scientific Speed Reading."

376. McKay, "How to Speed Read Like Theodore Roosevelt."

377. Klosowski, "The Truth about Speed Reading."

378. Ferriss, "Scientific Speed Reading."

379. Ibid.

380. Ibid.

381. McKay, "How to Speed Read Like Theodore Roosevelt."

382. Ferriss, "Scientific Speed Reading."

383. McKay, "How to Speed Read Like Theodore Roosevelt."

384. Cited in Ibid.

385. Klosowski, "The Truth about Speed Reading."

386. Mortimer Jerome Adler and Charles Lincoln Van Doren, *How to Read a Book*, Revised and updated edition (New York: Simon and Schuster, 1972).

387. Ibid.

388. Ibid.

389. Ibid.

390. Ibid.

391. Ibid.

392. Ibid., 36.

393. Ibid., 163–164.

394. Ibid.

395. Ibid.

396. Ibid.

397. Bruce Harpham, "16 Skills to Make Your Reading More Productive," *Lifehack*, n.d., http://www.lifehack.org/articles/productivity/16-skills-make-your-reading-more-productive.html.

398. "Reading a Textbook for True Understanding," *Cornell College*, accessed October 16, 2016, http://www.cornellcollege.edu/academic-support-and-advising/study-tips/reading-textbooks.shtml.

399. Ibid.

400. Ibid.

401. Shane Parrish, "The Top 3 Most Effective Ways to Take Notes While Reading," *Farnam Street*, November 26, 2013, https://

www.farnamstreetblog.com/2013/11/taking-notes-while-reading/.

402. Jonathan Milligan, "A Simple Guide to Indexing the Books You Read for Evernote," *JonathanMilligan.com*, June 4, 2014, http://jonathanmilligan.com/a-simple-guide-to-indexing-the-books-you-read-for-evernote/.

403. Harpham, "16 Skills To Make Your Reading More Productive."

404. Bert Webb, "Twelve Ways to Mark Up a Book," *Open Loops*, February 20, 2006, http://hwebbjr.typepad.com/openloops/2006/02/twelve_ways_to_.html.

405. Alexis Grant, "11 Ways to Take Notes While Reading," *Real-Time Chat for Online Hiring and Networking*, April 28, 2010, http://www.brazen.com/blog/archive/smart-hacks/11-ways-to-take-notes-while-reading/.

406. Webb, "Twelve Ways to Mark up a Book"; Shane Parrish, "The Best Way to Take Notes While Reading," April 29, 2014, http://theweek.com/articles/448549/best-way-take-notes-reading.

407. Ferriss, *Tools of Titans*.

408. Webb, "Twelve Ways to Mark Up a Book."

409. Grant, "11 Ways to Take Notes While Reading"; Webb, "Twelve Ways to Mark Up a Book."

410. Webb, "Twelve Ways to Mark Up a Book."

411. Grant, "11 Ways to Take Notes While Reading."

412. Ibid.

413. "Close Reading," Wikipedia, November 15, 2017, https://en.wikipedia.org/w/index.php?title=Close_reading&oldid=810524411.

414. Cornell College, "How to Read Closely: Making Sense out of Novels," *Cornell College*, accessed November 5, 2016, http://www.cornellcollege.edu/academic-support-and-advising/study-tips/reading-closely.shtml.

415. Ibid., A Closer Examination.

416. Milligan, "A Simple Guide to Indexing the Books You Read for Evernote."

417. Parrish, "The Best Way to Take Notes While Reading."

418. "Note-Taking for Reading," Skills You Need, accessed September 17, 2016, http://www.skillsyouneed.com/write/notes-reading.html.

419. Rainie et al., "The Rise of E-Reading."

420. M. Tanner, "Digital vs. Print: Reading Comprehension and the Future of the Book," *SJSU School of Information Student Research Journal* 4, no. 2 (December 19, 2014), http://scholarworks.sjsu.edu/slissrj/vol4/iss2/6.

421. Taylor Pipes, "Timeless Note-Taking Systems for Students," *Evernote Blog*, July 7, 2016, https://blog.evernote.com/blog/2016/07/07/timeless-note-taking-systems-for-students/.

422. Cited in Tanner, "Digital vs. Print."

423. Grant, "11 Ways to Take Notes While Reading."

424. Harpham, "16 Skills to Make Your Reading More Productive."

425. Ryan Holiday, "How and Why to Keep a 'Commonplace Book,'" *Thought Catalog*, August 28, 2013, http://thoughtcatalog.com/ryan-holiday/2013/08/how-and-why-to-keep-a-commonplace-book/. What Is a Commonplace Book?

426. Pipes, "Taking Note," February 26, 2016.

427. Pipes, "Taking Note," February 26, 2016, Applying Commonplace in Modern Times.

428. Juma, "What Is a Commonplace Book & Why You Need One."

429. Holiday, "How and Why to Keep a 'Commonplace Book.'"

430. Ryder Carroll, "Bullet Journal," *Bullet Journal*, 2016, http://bulletjournal.com/.

431. Ibid.

432. Jamie Miller, "8 Ways I Use My Bullet Journal as a Reader and a Blogger," *The Perpetual Page-Turner*, September 2, 2016, http://www.perpetualpageturner.com/2016/09/8-ways-i-use-my-bullet-journal-as-a-reader-a-blogger.html.

433. Tirzah Price, "Cool Bookish Ideas for Your Bullet Journal," *BOOK RIOT*, August 11, 2016, http://bookriot.com/2016/08/11/cool-bookish-ideas-bullet-journal/.

434. Miller, "8 Ways I Use My Bullet Journal as a Reader and a Blogger."

435. Ibid.

436. King, "6 Practical Tips to Help You Cultivate a Reading Habit."; Miller, "8 Ways I Use My Bullet Journal as a Reader and a Blogger"; Price, "Cool Bookish Ideas for Your Bullet Journal."

437. Susan Page, "Ronald Reagan's Note Card Collection Being Published," *USATODAY.COM*, May 8, 2011, http://www.usatoday.com/news/washington/2011-05-08-reagan-notes-book-brinkley_n.htm.

438. Ryan Holiday, "The Notecard System: The Key for Remembering, Organizing and Using Everything You Read," RyanHoliday.net, April 1, 2014, http://ryanholiday.net/the-notecard-system-the-key-for-remembering-organizing-and-using-everything-you-read/.

439. Ibid.

440. Ibid., The System.

441. Webb, "Twelve Ways to Mark Up a Book."

442. Tony Cortes, "Invest Learn Teach—Powerful Method to Build Authority," *Tony Cortes* (blog), February 2, 2016, http://www.tonycortes.com/invest-learn-teach/.

443. Ron Deering, "Ray Higdons ILT Method for Blogging," *Ron Deering* (blog), March 9, 2015, https://rondeering.com/ray-higdons-ilt-method-for-blogging/.

444. Besse, "The Philosophy of Reading."

445. Tanner, "Digital vs. Print."

446. Maria Konnikova, "Being a Better Online Reader," *The New Yorker*, July 16, 2014, http://www.newyorker.com/science/maria-konnikova/being-a-better-online-reader.

447. McLean, "Learning on the Margins of Adult Education."

448. Tanner, "Digital vs. Print."

449. Ibid. 4.

450. Zickuhr and Rainie, "E-Reading Rises as Device Ownership Jumps."

451. Andrew Dillon, "Reading from Paper versus Screens: A Critical Review of the Empirical Literature," *Ergonomics* 35, no. 10 (October 1992): 1297–1326, doi:10.1080/00140139208967394.

452. Alexandra Alter, "The Plot Twist: E-book Sales Slip, and Print Is far from Dead," *The New York Times*, September 22, 2015, http:// www.nytimes.com/2015/09/23/business/media/the-plot-twist-e-book-sales-slip-and-print-is-far-from-dead.html; Simon Jenkins, "Books Are Back. Only the Technodazzled Thought They Would Go Away," *The Guardian*, May 13, 2016, sec. Opinion, https://www.theguardian.com/commentisfree/2016/may/13/books-e-book-publishers-paper.

453. "Millennials Want to Make Books Cool Again."

454. Alter, "The Plot Twist."

455. Jenkins, "Books Are Back: Only the Technodazzled Thought They Would Go Away," para. 12.

456. Alex Gladu, "Why Reading a Print Book Is Better for You and for Main Street," *Independent We Stand*, May 10, 2016, http:// www.independentwestand.org/blog-reading-a-print-book-is-better-for-you/.

457. Grate, "Science Has Great News for People Who Read Actual Books."; Myrberg and Wiberg, "Screen vs. Paper."

458. Konnikova, "Being a Better Online Reader."

459. Myrberg and Wiberg, "Screen vs. Paper"; Tanner, "Digital vs. Print"; Wise, "8 Science-Backed Reasons to Read a (Real) Book."

460. Ferris Jabr, "The Reading Brain in the Digital Age: The Science of Paper versus Screens," *Scientific American*, April 11, 2013, https:// www.scientificamerican.com/article/reading-paper-screens/.

461. Tanner, "Digital vs. Print."

462. Dillon, "Reading from Paper versus Screens."

463. Myrberg and Wiberg, "Screen vs. Paper."

464. Cited in Jabr, "The Reading Brain in the Digital Age."

465. Victoria Marsick and Karen Watkins, *Informal and Incidental Learning in the Workplace* (London;New York: Routledge, 1990).

466. Ibid.

467. Anne Niccoli, "Paper or Tablet? Reading Recall and Comprehension," *EDUCAUSE Review*, September 28, 2015, http://er.educause.edu/articles/2015/9/paper-or-tablet-reading-recall-and-comprehension.

468. Cited in Tanner, "Digital vs. Print."

469. Ibid., 2.

470. Ibid.

471. Zickuhr and Rainie, "E-Reading Rises as Device Ownership Jumps."

472. Ibid. 11.

473. Ibid.

474. Rainie et al., "The Rise of E-Reading."

475. Alter, "The Plot Twist."
476. Myrberg and Wiberg, "Screen vs. Paper."
477. Rainie et al., "The Rise of E-Reading."
478. Levin, "How to Read More Books: Benefits of Reading." Section: How to Read More.
479. Rainie et al., "The Rise of E-Reading."
480. Dillon, "Reading from Paper versus Screens."
481. Ibid.
482. Myrberg and Wiberg, "Screen vs. Paper."
483. Ibid.
484. Ibid.
485. Cited in Tanner, "Digital vs. Print."
486. Myrberg and Wiberg, "Screen vs. Paper"; Tanner, "Digital vs. Print."
487. Tanner, "Digital vs. Print."
488. Foasberg, "Adoption of E-Book Readers Among College Students."
489. Niccoli, "Paper or Tablet? Reading Recall and Comprehension."
490. Zickuhr and Rainie, "E-Reading Rises as Device Ownership Jumps."
491. Corley, "Reading Habits of the Affluent."
492. Brian Tracy, "5 Ways to Gain a Competitive Advantage: The Importance of Continuous Learning and Personal Development," *Brian Tracy's Blog*, October 11, 2012, http://www.briantracy.com/blog/personal-success/5-ways-to-gain-a-competitive-advantage-the-importance-of-continuous-learning-and-personal-development/.
493. Vozza, "Why You Should Read 50 Books This Year (and How to Do It)."
494. Parrish, "What You Didn't Know about the Act of Reading Books."
495. Patrick Bet-David, "How to Choose the Right Books to Read," *Patrick Bet-David* (blog), September 13, 2016, http://www.patrickbetdavid.com/choose-the-right-books-to-read/; Harpham, "16 Skills To Make Your Reading More Productive."
496. Kelly, *The Inevitable*.
497. Rainie et al., "The Rise of E-Reading," p. 7.
498. Miller, Purcell, and Rainie, "Reading Habits in Different Communities."
499. Rainie et al., "The Rise of E-Reading."
500. Caitlin White, "U.S. Independent Bookstores Thriving, despite Major Declines across the Pond," Bustle, February 26, 2015, http://www.bustle.com/articles/66629-us-independent-bookstores-thriving-despite-major-declines-across-the-pond.
501. Kristen Swanson, *Professional Learning in the Digital Age: The Educator's Guide to User-Generated Learning* (Larchmont, NY: Eye on Education, 2013).
502. Stager, "Everything I Know about Reading Instruction I Learned from Oprah Winfrey."
503. Heidi Bahnck, "How to Pick Books to Read," *Pro Book Club*, May 1, 2014, http://probookclub.com/how-to-pick-books-to-read/.

504. Miller, Purcell, and Rainie, "Reading Habits in Different Communities."

505. Lee Rainie, "7 Surprises about Libraries in Our Surveys," *Pew Research Center*, June 30, 2014, http://www.pewresearch.org/fact-tank/2014/06/30/7-surprises-about-libraries-in-our-surveys/. Section 2.

506. Miller, Purcell, and Rainie, "Reading Habits in Different Communities."

507. Rainie, "7 Surprises about Libraries in Our Surveys."

508. Ibid., Section 2.

509. Kathryn Zickuhr, Kristen Purcell, and Lee Rainie, "From Distance Admirers to Library Lovers—and Beyond" (Washington, D.C.: Pew Research Center, March 2014), http://www.pewinternet.org/files/2014/03/PIP-Library-Typology-Report_031314.pdf, p. 4.

510. Ibid.

511. Tanner, "Digital vs. Print."

512. Miller, Purcell, and Rainie, "Reading Habits in Different Communities."

513. Kathryn Zickuhr and Maeve Duggan, "E-book Reading Jumps; Print Book Reading Declines" (Washington, D.C.: Pew Research Center, December 27, 2012), http://libraries.pewinternet.org/files/legacy-pdf/PIP_Reading%20and%20e-books_12.27.pdf; Zickuhr and Rainie, "E-Reading Rises as Device Ownership Jumps."

514. Miller, Purcell, and Rainie, "Reading Habits in Different Communities."

515. Parrish, "The Best Way to Find More Time to Read."

516. Rainie, "7 Surprises about Libraries in Our Surveys," Section 5.

517. Rainie et al., "The Rise of E-Reading."

518. John Maher, "Audiobook Revenue Jumped 22.7% in 2018," PublishersWeekly.com, June 21, 2018, https://www.publishersweekly.com/pw/by-topic/industry-news/audio-books/article/77303-audiobook-revenue-jumped-22-7-in-2018.html.

519. Kaisja Calkins, April 19, 2016, Facebook post.

520. Austin, "'Billionaire' Reading Habits: 11 Ways to Read 52 Books in 52 Weeks, 2X Your Reading Speed and Improve Your Comprehension by 500%."

521. Ibid., 10. Think Like a Cave-man.

522. Simmons, "9 Creative Ways to Find Books That Will Make You a Genius."

523. Emily VanBuren, "7 Apps for Cataloguing Your Home Library," *Inside HigherEd*, June 12, 2014, https://www.insidehighered.com/blogs/gradhacker/7-apps-cataloguing-your-home-library#sthash.XJwyHHQF.Tuj4REbV.dpbs.

524. Jay Cross, *Informal Learning: Rediscovering the Natural Pathways That Inspire Innovation and Performance* (San Francisco, CA: John Wiley, 2007); Eija Korpelainen and Mari Kira, "Employees' Choices in Learning How to Use Information and Communication Technology Systems at Work: Strategies and Approaches," *International Journal of Training and Development* 14, no. 1 (March 2010): 32–53, doi:10.1111/j.1468-2419.2009.00339.x; Daniel Tobin, *All Learning Is Self-Directed: How Organizations Can Support and Encourage Independent Learning* (Alexandria VA: ASTD, 2000).

525. Lance Dublin, "Formalizing Informal Learning," *Chief Learning Officer* 9, no.

3 (2010): 20–23.

526. Graham Attwell, "Web 2.0 and the Changing Ways We Are Using Computers for Learning: What Are the Implications for Pedagogy and Curriculum?," April 6, 2010, http://citeseerx.ist.psu.edu/viewdoc/download? doi=10.1.1.122.6064&rep=rep1&type=pdf; Allen M Tough, *Why Adults Learn: A Study of the Major Reasons for Beginning and Continuing a Learning Project.* (Toronto: Ontario Inst. for Studies in Education, 1968), http:// search.ebscohost.com.proxy.uwlib.uwyo.edu/login.aspx? direct=true&db=eric&AN=ED025688&site=ehost-live.

527. Malcolm Knowles, *The Modern Practice of Adult Education: From Pedagogy to Andragogy*, Rev. and Updated. (Wilton, Conn. ;Chicago, Ill: Association Press; Follett Pub. Co., 1980).

528. Russell Ackoff and Daniel Greenberg, *Turning Learning Right Side Up: Putting Education Back on Track* (Upper Saddle River, NJ: Wharton, 2008); Knowles, *The Modern Practice of Adult Education: From Pedagogy to Andragogy*; Marsick and Watkins, *Informal and Incidental Learning in the Workplace*; George Siemens, *Knowing Knowledge* (Lexington, KY, 2006), http://www.elearnspace.org/ KnowingKnowledge_LowRes.pdf.

529. Siemens, *Knowing Knowledge.*

530. Ibid.

531. Dublin, "Formalizing Informal Learning."

532. Attwell, "Web 2.0 and the Changing Ways We Are Using Computers for Learning: What Are the Implications for Pedagogy and Curriculum?"; Tobin, *All Learning Is Self-Directed: How Organizations Can Support and Encourage Independent Learning.*

533. Cross, *Informal Learning: Rediscovering the Natural Pathways That Inspire Innovation and Performance.*

534. Tobin, *All Learning Is Self-Directed: How Organizations Can Support and Encourage Independent Learning.*

535. Nick Shackleton-Jones, "Informal Learning and the Future.," *Training Journal*, 2008, 38–41.

536. Nancy Day, "Informal Learning Gets Results," *Workforce* 77, no. 6 (June 1998): 30–36.

537. Ibid.; Allen Tough, *Intentional Changes: A Fresh Approach to Helping People Change* (Chicago IL.: Follett, 1982).

538. Allen Tough, *Intentional Changes: A Fresh Approach to Helping People Change* (Chicago Ill.: Follett Pub. Co., 1982).

539. Vincent Belliveau, "The Industrialisation of Informal Learning," *Training Journal*, 2010, 50–53.

540. Agatha Gilmore, "Hands Off: Facilitating Informal Learning," *Certification Magazine* 10, no. 10 (2008): 46–49; Tobin, *All Learning Is Self-Directed: How Organizations Can Support and Encourage Independent Learning.*

541. Tobin, *All Learning Is Self-Directed: How Organizations Can Support and En-*

courage Independent Learning.

542. Ibid.

543. Ibid.

544. Knowles, *The Modern Practice of Adult Education: From Pedagogy to Andragogy.*

545. Ibid.; Tobin, *All Learning Is Self-Directed: How Organizations Can Support and Encourage Independent Learning.*

546. Chip R Bell, "Informal Learning in Organizations," *Personnel J*, no. 6 (1977): 280; Kelsey Meyer, "Why Leaders Must Be Readers," *Forbes*, August 3, 2012, http://www.forbes.com/sites/85broads/2012/08/03/why-leaders-must-be-readers/#483f766d6563.

547. Jim Greer, "Want More Military Leaders Reading? Use the Pabst Blue Ribbon Strategy," *From the Green Note-book*, July 16, 2015, https://fromthegreennote-book.com/2015/07/16/want-more-military-leaders-reading-use-the-pabst-blue-ribbon-strategy/.

548. Coleman, "For Those Who Want to Lead, Read"; Greer, "Want More Military Leaders Reading?"; Meyer, "Why Leaders Must Be Readers."

549. Sid T. Womack and B. J. Chandler, "Encouraging Reading for Professional Development," *Journal of Reading* 35, no. 5 (February 1992): 390.

550. Ibid.

551. Ibid.

552. Tobin, *All Learning Is Self-Directed: How Organizations Can Support and Encourage Independent Learning.*

553. Ronald R. Fogleman, "CSAF Professional Reading Program," *Airpower Journal* 11, no. 1 (Spring 1997): 63–65. p. 63.

554. Ibid. p. 64.

555. "The U.S. Army Chief of Staff Professional Reading List" (U.S. Army Center of Military History, n.d.), http://www.history.army.mil/html/books/105/105-1-1/CMH_Pub_105-5-1_2013.pdf, p. 3.

556. Parrish, "Jeff Bezos's Reading List."

557. Greer, "Want More Military Leaders Reading?"

558. Halelly Azulay, "5 Ways to Develop Employees without Spending a Dime," Association for Talent Development, September 17, 2012, https://www.td.org/Publications/Blogs/Management-Blog/2012/09/5-Ways-to-Develop-Employees-Without-Spending-a-Dime; Marsick and Watkins, *Informal and Incidental Learning in the Workplace.*

559. Greer, "Want More Military Leaders Reading?"

560. Byerly, "Use 'Mental Models' to Outthink the Enemy."

561. Marine Corps Association and Foundation, "MCA&F's Unit Libraries: 'Giving the Marine a "No Excuse" Opportunity to Complete Their Reading,'" *Marine Corps Association and Foundation*, January 8, 2016, https://www.mcafdn.org/gallery/mcafs-unit-libraries-giving-marine-no-excuse-opportunity-complete-their-reading.

562. Paul Corrigan, "Students, Keep Your Books," *Inside Higher Ed*, June 3, 2016,

https://www.insidehighered.com/views/2016/06/03/enduring-power-textbooks-students-lives-essay.

563. Ibid.

564. Ibid.

565. Kelly, *The Inevitable.* p. 204.

566. Ryan Holiday, "How to Keep a Library of (Physical) Books," *Thought Catalog* (blog), September 17, 2013, http://thoughtcatalog.com/ryan-holiday/2013/09/how-to-keep-a-library-of-physical-books/. para. 24.

567. David Alves, "How to Build Your Personal Library," *David's Place* (blog), September 20, 2011, https://davidcalves.com/2011/09/20/how-to-build-your-personal-library/; Leah French, "How to Create a Home Library Using Flea Market Finds," The Spruce, accessed October 7, 2018, https://www.thespruce.com/how-to-create-a-home-library-1313432.

568. French, "How to Create a Home Library Using Flea Market Finds."

569. Alves, "How to Build Your Personal Library."

570. Holiday, "How to Keep a Library of (Physical) Books."

571. Edmonds, "How to Create a Home Library."

572. Weller, *The Digital Scholar.*

573. Ibid.

574. Stager, "Everything I Know about Reading Instruction I Learned from Oprah Winfrey."

575. J. Jefferson Looney, "Number of Letters Jefferson Wrote," *The Jefferson Monticello*, March 24, 2008, https://www.monticello.org/site/research-and-collections/number-letters-jefferson-wrote.

576. Ibid.

577. Franklin and Smith, *Autobiography of Benjamin Franklin.*

578. "Adams Electronic Archive: Diary of John Adams," *Massachusetts Historical Society*, accessed May 20, 2016, http://www.masshist.org/digitaladams/archive/diary/.

579. Jean McCormick, "Would Thomas Jefferson Have Tweeted?," *BraveNew*, October 17, 2013, https://bravenew.com/blog/2013/10/17/would-thomas-jefferson-have-tweeted/.

580. Jonathan Lyons, "Benjamin Franklin: America's First Social Networker?," *Science Friday*, July 4, 2013, http://www.sciencefriday.com/articles/benjamin-franklin-americas-first-social-networker/.

581. Ibid.

582. Harpham, "16 Skills To Make Your Reading More Productive."

583. Austin, "'Billionaire' Reading Habits: 11 Ways to Read 52 Books in 52 Weeks, 2X Your Reading Speed and Improve Your Comprehension by 500%."

REDSCORPION
—— PRESS ——

Red Scorpion Press was formed in January 2016 with the hope of bettering the world in a small way through publishing. Our aim is to push boundaries and be an outlet for fresh voices and unique perspectives that entertain and inform.

Please visit us at www.redscorpionpress.com for our latest selection of books.

Printed in the USA
CPSIA information can be obtained
at www.ICGtesting.com
LVHW020855281123
765150LV00045B/1759